Watch it...Do it™

Great Cooking Made Easy

watchitdoit.com

Thankyou to everyone in our production team at Williams Media Publishing Ltd and

Cover and Principal Photography	Phil at Phil Boorman Photography
Copy Editors	Hilary McGlynn
	Katie Hunt
Production Editor	Mirjana Misina
Nutritionist	Fiona Hunter
Design & Layout	Andrew Buxton at Williams Media Publishing Ltd

Special thanks also to Jane Holdsworth at the Food & Drink Federation, Sheila Lambie at Oxford Brookes University and Roy Clark.

First published in 2007 by Williams Media Publishing Ltd

Disclaimer

The recipes and ingredients recommended for the dishes contained in this book are aimed at healthy individuals and are not specific to any individuals or their particular circumstances. Always check the list of ingredients for each specific dish. If you are in any doubt as to whether an ingredient is appropriate for you, you should consult your GP. You are wholly responsible for checking each recipe to ensure that it meets your needs. Do not use any ingredients you think you may have an allergy to.

ISBN: 978-0-9554953-0-4

Printed in the UK by CPI Bath Press

www.williamsmp.com

Watch it...Do it™

Our Promise

Thank you for choosing to buy *Cooking for Kids Made Easy*.

I created this product because I am a self-confessed 'can't cook' and I found cookery books impossible to use – they have only a few photos and the text is difficult to follow. They just don't seem to be designed to really help you make the recipes.

I believed that there just had to be a better and easier way to make great food!

For me, the best way to understand how to make a recipe is to first watch it being made and then to use a simple step-by-step guide to help make it. We had just created the **Watch it...Do it**™ format!

We made a DVD video and book demo and it worked! We even tested **Watch It...Do It**™ on me, to make sure it was completely fool-proof. It was! I made food way beyond my skill level, it was easy, tasted great and was stress free – my girlfriend just couldn't believe it!

Our promise is that we will always go that extra mile to help you make great food and we'll make it as easy to do as possible – easier than any ordinary cookbook. I promise you, we care that you will be able make the food in our titles. We'll leave no stone unturned.

I hope that you too discover that there is no easier way to make great food than **Watch it...Do it**™. Don't forget to let us know what you think by visiting our website and posting your comments at **watchitdoit.com**

I look forward to hearing from you and thanks again.

Jason Williams
Self confessed 'can't cook' & founder of **Watch it...Do it**™

PS. Don't forget to visit www.watchitdoit.com for FREE recipes!

Special thanks to Sasha and Megan for being the **Watch it...Do it**™ stars.

Thank you girls!

Contents

Step-by-step recipes

Introduction

Cooking for Kids Made Easy is a step-by-step guide to helping mums and dads cook great food for their kids.

We felt that there wasn't enough help for mums and dads who need an easy way to cook good food for their kids in a world where we all seem to work longer and have less time to enjoy some of what life has to offer.

With our unique **Watch It...Do It**™ format, we'll make it easy for you, no matter what your cookery skills – whether you're a novice or a master chef – to cook for your kids.

First you'll be able to watch a step-by-step video for every recipe. The recipe videos show you exactly what you need to do to make the dish in easy-to-understand and easy-to-follow steps.

Then the step-by-step book will help you to cook the recipes in your own kitchen, reminding you what you have just watched on the DVD. Simply follow each step until the recipe is complete – it couldn't be easier!

We have also included some key nutritional informational to help you learn about how to make sure your kids are eating a balanced diet. It covers the basics so you can start to make decisions that affect your kids' diet in a positive way right now.

Cooking for Kids Made Easy isn't about stopping the sweets and treats kids love so much and forcing them to eat sticks of celery all the time! It's about giving them a balanced diet, which is why we have also included for every recipe the Guideline Daily Amounts (GDAs) that will help you maintain a balanced diet for your family. We're not going to tell you what to feed your kids' – that's up to you – but we do think we can help you learn new recipes easier than any ordinary cookbook.

The GDAs are a great guide for parents to monitor their kids' diet. More information is available on our website at watchitdoit.com, where you'll find loads of free stuff.

Using the DVD

Choose your disc

To watch the recipes insert either of the discs into your DVD player or PC.

- **Disc 1** contains the *Breakfasts* and *Treats*
- **Disc 2** contains the *Tea Time* recipes
- Then go to the appropriate menu and select the recipe you are interested in making

Watching a recipe

- You will be able to watch a preview of the recipe and then decide whether you are going to watch it step-by-step or all at once
- When you watch it step-by-step, you can watch the video as often as you like and repeat the steps if you need to

Making a recipe

- Now you've watched the video you are ready to make the recipe
- Find the recipe you want to make in the book and follow the steps in your kitchen

It couldn't be simpler!

We were lucky to have Colin Gray as our expert chef for *Cooking for Kids Made Easy* because, if he isn't cooking for the Queen, he's busy competing for the Welsh national culinary team all over the world!

Colin has spent his entire life cooking and now owns an award-winning catering company and a concept restauarant. He also competes as a chef for his country and is a consultant chef to the Welsh Assembly.

In between this, we managed to persuade him to cook some great recipes for us!

Colin is no stranger to the Queen, having cooked for Her Majesty on numerous occasions, including the last three Parliamentary openings in Cardiff. Prince Charles has also enjoyed Colin's cooking at his private parties while he is in residence at Highgrove.

Whilst representing his country, Colin has won Gold, Silver and Bronze medals for his food. His catering company won Best Catering Company in Wales two years in a row in 2004 and 2005.

The inspiration for his kids' recipes has been a pragmatic approach to a balanced diet. Colin calls it 'Real food for real mums and dads.'

'I loved putting the recipes together for this title – I couldn't believe how simple **Watch It...Do It**™ have made cooking! It also felt great to be giving real mums and dads easy to learn cookery skills that can help them give their kids the balanced diet they need.'

Breakfast

3 Real Fruit Smoothies

Malted Banana, Strawberry & Raspberry; Fruit Tango

Smoothies are healthy, fun and quick to prepare, which makes them ideal for breakfasts on the run! Page 36

Boiled Eggs

with Cheese and Ham Soldiers

A tasty twist on the classic kids' favourite, with ham and cheddar cheese soldiers for dipping. Page 42

Supreme Scrambled Eggs

Creamy scrambled eggs served on a hot toasted muffin. Page 45

Poached Eggs

This clever way of poaching eggs will be great fun and guarantee you the perfect poached egg every time! Page 49

RATING

Full English Breakfast

This recipe simplifies and cuts down the amount of work usually needed for an English breakfast. Cooking on a grilling rack will reduce the amount of fat normally found in an English breakfast. Page 52

Porridge Plus

with 3 Great Toppings

A classic, healthy, home-made breakfast – we have given you some suggestions to make it more exciting. Strawberries and brown sugar, apricots and almonds, bananas and hazelnuts – a great slow release of energy to start the day! Page 56

RATING

Home-Roasted Cereal

with 3 Great Toppings

This great home-made cereal mix can be made in larger amounts and then stored in the fridge for up to 3 months. Packed with fruit and nuts, try it topped with Greek yoghurt and honey, crème fraîche and blueberry or orange and chocolate milk! Page 62

RATING   

Breakfast Muffins and Crumpets

Muffins and crumpets are great topped with a whole range of sweet and savoury ingredients; brie, bacon and tomato, mixed berries and yoghurt and peanut butter with banana. Page 68

RATING   

Sweet French Toast

Crispy on the outside and gooey in the middle – wonderfully finished with cinnamon, sugar and maple syrup. Page 74

RATING   

Savoury French Toast

Savoury French toast can be just as tasty as sweet. This simple, tasty breakfast dish is given an extra twist by the sweet cherry tomatoes. Page 78

Welsh Rarebit

The original cheese on toast! Always a favourite with the kids, but be careful not to add too much mustard! You can also make Buck Rarebit – just add a poached egg on top at the end!
Page 83

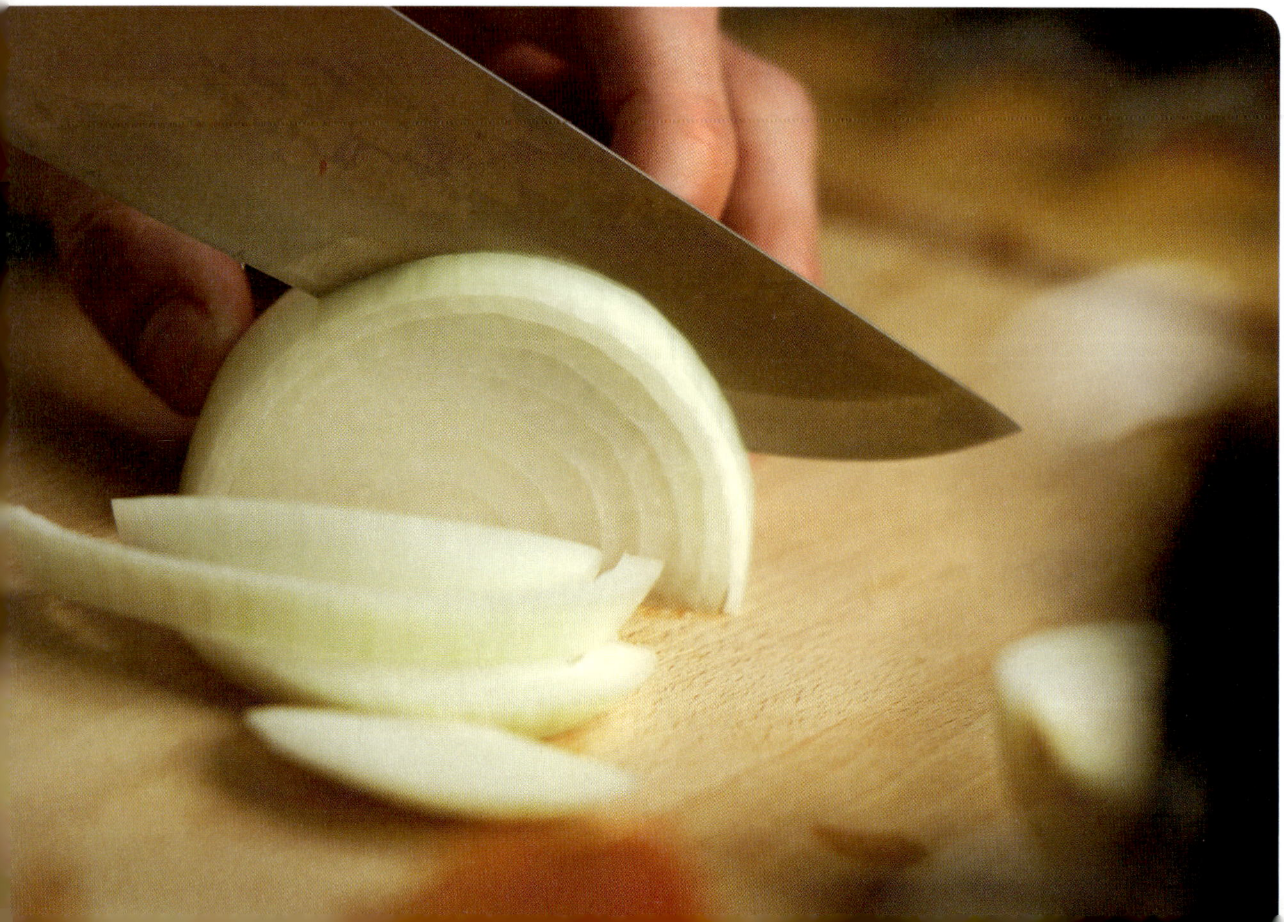

Tea Time

Home-Made Fish Fingers *with Peas and Home-Made Tartar Sauce*

Pure 100% fresh fish coated in fresh breadcrumbs, served with peas and a piquant home-made tartar sauce. Page 90

Batterless Fish *and Oven-Baked Chunky Chips*

A very light coating of thin, crispy batter and oven-baked chunky chips make this famous dish a healthier alternative. Page 98

Home-Made Beef Burgers *with Home-Made Tomato Sauce*

100% pure lean minced beef, nothing added. Served with our home-made tomato sauce and lots of salad. Leave out the cheese for a healthier burger. Page 104

Spicy Crumbed Chicken Nuggets

100% chicken breast with a Chinese five-spice coating, served with fresh spinach and our special BBQ sauce. Spicy Crumbed Chicken Nuggets are a healthier alternative to their ready-made counterparts and are guaranteed to delight your children. Page 112

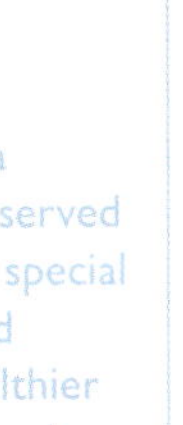

RATING

Home-Made Bangers *and Creamy Mash with Home-Made Chunky Onion Gravy*

The classic British dish utilising home-made pork, sage and onion sausages, creamy mash and healthy onion gravy. Page 119

Oven-Baked Pork Meatballs *with Fresh Tomato Sauce*

Fresh pork, onion and garlic meatballs oven-baked in a home-made tomato sauce. Page 130

Smoked Haddock and Pea Fish Cakes

with Stir-Fried Pak Choi

East meets West with a classic fish cake containing peas, served with stir-fried pak choi. Page 139

RATING

Lasagne Pots

Individual portions of lean minced beef, pasta and creamy cheese sauce served with crusty bread. Page 148

RATING

Super Thin Pizzas

with 3 Toppings

A favourite thin and crispy pizza base topped with mushroom and thyme, Cajun chicken and sweetcorn, or ham, onion and tomato. Page 156

RATING

Honey and Lemon Chicken Kebabs

with Garlic Bread

A healthy and tasty way of using chicken thighs with a honey, lemon and plum marinade, served with classic garlic bread. Page 172

RATING

Veggie Kids' Kebabs

with Coconut Rice

Grilled vegetarian kebabs with a garlic marinade, served with coconut basmati rice and plum sauce. Page 180

RATING

Chicken Piri Piri Kebabs

with a Crunchy Thai Salad

A zingy marinade of lemon, sweet chilli and plum make these kebabs extra interesting – served with a Thai-style salad. Page 187

RATING

Veggie Lasagne

The ultimate 5-a-day dish. Use any combination of fresh vegetables to create this vegetarian version of the classic Italian dish. Page 194

Macaroni Cheese Bake

Oven-baked pasta with basil and garlic, coated with a creamy cheese sauce and topped with fresh breadcrumbs and Parmesan for extra crunch. Page 206

Spag Bol

The classic Italian staple – made even easier! Page 214

Fusilli Carbonara

Classic Italian energy burst with sugar snaps, bacon and garlic. Page 221

RATING

Hi-Five Pasta

Get your 5-a-day here. Fresh tagliatelle with 5 varieties of vegetables cunningly hidden in a tomato sauce. Page 226

Beef Stew and Dumplings

A British winter warmer with lean braising steak, lots of vegetables and bacon-and-onion-flavoured dumplings. Page 235

RATING

Haddock and Prawn Smokies

Poached haddock and king prawns in a creamy cheese sauce, served in individual pots with a tangy watercress salad. If you want a stronger flavour, use the milk you used to cook the fish in to make the cheese sauce! Page 247

RATING

Tomato and Vegetable Noodles

A healthy noodle snack with fresh tomatoes, noodles and vegetable broth. Great served with soy sauce. Page 255

RATING

Chicken and Mushroom Noodles

A healthy noodle snack with fresh chicken breast, mushrooms, noodles and chicken broth, topped with spring onion. Page 260

RATING

BBQ Beef Noodles

A healthy noodle snack with fresh beef stock, hoisin sauce and beef broth. Page 266

RATING

Chicken Fajitas

Mexican food made easy! Fresh chicken breast with red pepper, chilli, tomatoes, paprika and sour cream. Page 272

RATING

Chilli Con Carne
with Cheesy Corn Chips

Sweet chilli sauce adds a new dimension to this classic Mexican chilli. Served with cheese-coated corn chips for an authentic taste. The sour cream dampens the spiciness. Page 279

RATING

Sausage Casserole

A one-pot casserole combining Cumberland sausage, fresh vegetables, apples and potatoes – ideal for supper. Page 284

Aromatic Lamb Burgers

with Crushed Spuds and Raita

A light flavouring of cumin, rosemary and sage provides these 100% lean lamb burgers with their aromatic taste. Served on crushed garlic new potatoes with home-made raita. Page 291

Hot Pot

The classic of all classics, using lean neck fillet of lamb and bundles of fresh vegetables, topped with thinly sliced potatoes and oven-baked. A great family dish! Page 299

Chicken Burgers

A healthy chicken burger, lightly flavoured with sage and onion, served on a toasted sesame bun with reduced-fat mayo and iceberg lettuce. Page 307

Treats

Chocolate Brownies

An American classic! Lightly spiced with cloves, ginger and cinnamon. Chopped walnuts provide the crunch. A great snack for children and adults alike!
Page 318

RATING   

Apple Pie

Classic home-made pie with piquant bramley apples and cinnamon. Great served hot or cold with cream, ice cream or custard.
Page 328

RATING   

Caramelised Rice Pudding

Hot, creamy rice pudding with real vanilla seeds, topped with caramelised muscavado sugar. A good tip is not to put the caster sugar in the rice pudding mix until right at the end, as the sugar is what can cause the pudding to burn on the bottom! Page 338

RATING     

Little Chocolate Mousse Pots

Rich dark chocolate pots topped with fluffy, whipped cream and a chocolate decoration. Make sure you use fresh, free-range eggs.
Page 342

RATING   

Orange & Marmalade Bread & Butter Pudding

A traditional favourite with fresh vanilla seeds, finished with orange marmalade. Page 349

RATING   

Honey & Pumpkin Seed Oaty Bars

A fruit-and-nut-style flapjack packed with oats. A great alternative snack that won't last long in the biscuit tin! Page 355

RATING  

Super Fruit Trifles

A colourful, fruity version of the traditional dessert with strawberries, blueberries and raspberries. Topped with freshly whipped cream. Page 366

RATING 

Giant Cookies

Gigantic chocolate chip cookies, crispy on the outside, gooey in the middle. Great served with a glass of cold milk! Page 372

RATING 

Lemon Loaf

A zingy, lemony, soft loaf cake with mixed peel and chopped nuts. A simple recipe that works every time. Page 378

RATING 

Healthy Eating for Kids

We all want to do the best for our children and when it comes to their health one of the most important things parents can do is to provide a healthy diet. Encouraging them to eat a balanced diet will help ensure that they get all the nutrients vital for growth and development as well as laying down the foundations for good health later in life. It's not just their long term health that will benefit from a balanced diet – new research suggests that what they eat can also affect their behaviour and concentration levels.

What is a healthy balanced diet?

It's important to remember that there are no 'good' or 'bad' foods; it is the overall combination that matters. Using the Guideline Daily Amounts (GDAs) is a great way to help you make sure you get the balance of the diet right for your kids. I am delighted to see that **Watch it...Do it**™ are including GDA values for every recipe in this book to help make it easier for you to give your kids the diet they need.

Children need many different nutrients to help them grow and stay healthy. Making sure they eat a varied diet, with foods from each of the following food groups, is the best way to ensure they get everything they need.

Grains, cereals, potatoes include all types of bread, pasta, rice, noodles, couscous, potatoes, sweet potatoes and breakfast cereals

- Children need 4 or more servings from this group each day
- Foods from this group should make up around a third of the food on the plate at each meal

Fruit and vegetables include fresh, frozen, canned fruits (in juice rather than syrup) and dried fruits

- Children over the age of 5 should be encouraged to eat at least 5 portions a day
- Try to make sure that children are given some fruit or vegetables at each meal
- Young children often find a huge pile of vegetables off putting. It's much better to give them an amount you know they will eat and gradually increase the portion size as they get older.

One portion/serving is approximately 80g which is equivalent to:

1 piece of fruit (e.g. apple, banana, pear)
2 small fruits (e.g. kiwi, plums, tangerines)
A handful of smaller fruit (grapes, cherries)
2–3 tablespoons of vegetables

1 small bowl of salad
2–3 tablespoons stewed or canned fruit
1 slice of a large fruit (e.g. melon)
1 small glass fruit juice*

** Fruit juice counts as only one portion, however much is consumed*

Milk and dairy foods include milk, cheese and yogurt. These foods are an important source of calcium, which is essential for growing bones.

- Children need 3–4 servings from this group a day, depending on their age
- One serving equals a glass of milk, a small pot of yogurt or a matchbox-size piece of cheese
- Children under the age of 2 should be given full-fat milk. After the age of 2 if your child has a good appetite, its OK to switch to semi-skimmed milk. From the age of 5, you can use semi-skimmed milk and reduced fat products

Meat, fish and alternatives include meat, fish, eggs, nuts and pulses. Foods in this group provide protein, iron and zinc as well as other minerals and some vitamins.

- Children eating meat and fish need 2 servings per day
- Vegetarian children who only eat eggs, nuts and pulses need 2–3 servings per day.

Foods high in fat and sugar should not be eaten too often, and when they are, only in small amounts. Foods and drinks containing sugar should be consumed mainly at mealtimes to reduce the risk of tooth decay.

Tips to help your kids to grow up healthily

1. Healthy, active children are more likely to grow into healthy active adults. It's important to help your children to be physically active. Ideally children need at least 30–60 minutes of physical activity every day. Physical activity doesn't have to be formal exercise – encourage active play such as throwing and catching games or skipping.
2. Try to maintain structured meal times and snacks rather than letting children graze continually throughout the day.
3. Don't let your children fill up on fizzy drinks or squash in between meals. Drinks can be very filling, which can reduce a child's appetite for healthy foods at meal times.
4. When your child says they are hungry, offer a piece of fruit first. Only when they've eaten that can they have something else.
5. Don't forget kids learn by example, so make sure you set a good one (if you eat a well-balanced diet too, kids are more likely to follow)

I hope that you find this introduction a useful guide and by buying **Watch it...Do it**™ *Cooking for Kids Made Easy* you're one step closer to getting your kids on the road to a balanced diet. Good luck!

Fiona Hunter

Fiona Hunter
Bsc (Hons) Nutrition, Dip Dietetics

Guideline Daily Amounts (GDAs)

Throughout the **Watch It...Do It**™ recipe book series you will find Guideline Daily Amount (GDA) information for all the tasty recipes provided – this will help you to know what's inside a portion of the recipe and how much this contributes towards a healthy diet.

Guideline Daily Amounts (GDAs) are quite simply a guide to the amount of energy and nutrients an average healthy person needs for a balanced diet. They can be used to take the guesswork out of what and how much we should be eating if we want to stay healthy.

Let's take calories, for example. We all know that we need a certain amount of calories a day (around 2000 for the average adult/ 1800 for the average child).

But calories aren't the only thing that you may want to keep an eye on in your diet. There are also Guideline Daily Amounts for other key nutrients such as sugars, fat, saturates and salt.

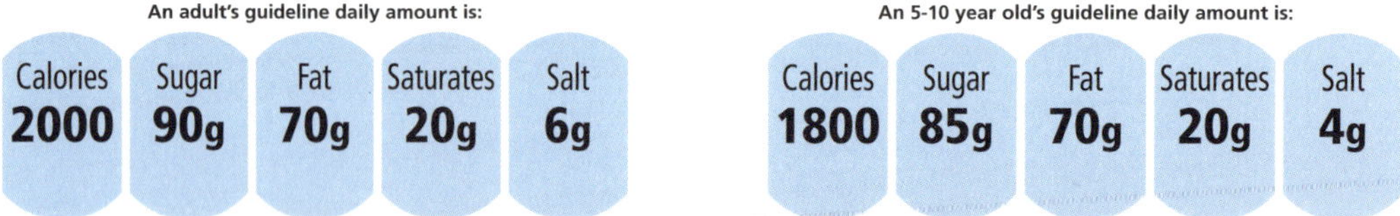

Its also worth noting that GDAs aren't a target but a guide. Whilst it's OK to stick pretty close to your GDA for calories, you should really aim to eat no more than your GDA for the other four nutirients - sugar, fat, saturates and salt.

Here's how our GDA labels work:

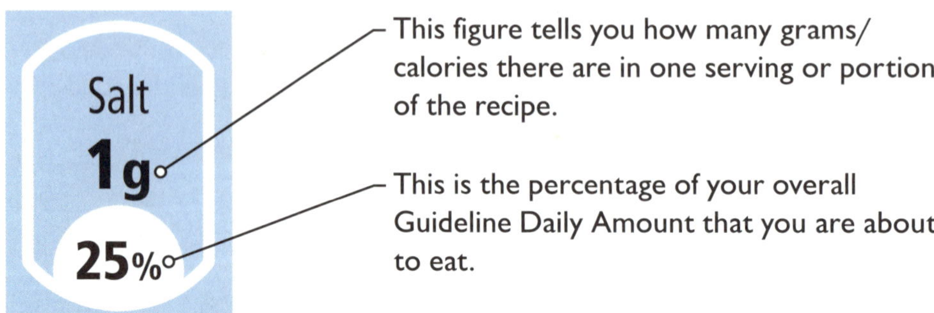

By turning all those numbers into percentages – figures out of a hundred – we've done all the hard work for you. Because now you can see at a glance how much of your Guideline Daily Amounts are in each of our recipes.

Here's an example from the Tomato and Vegetable Noodles recipe in *Cooking for Kids Made Easy*.

A typical serving contains (based on the max. number of people this recipe serves):

Calories	Sugar	Fat	Saturates	Salt
314	**6.0g**	**11g**	**2.0g**	**1.0g**
17%	**7%**	**16%**	**10%**	**25%**

of a child's guideline daily amount

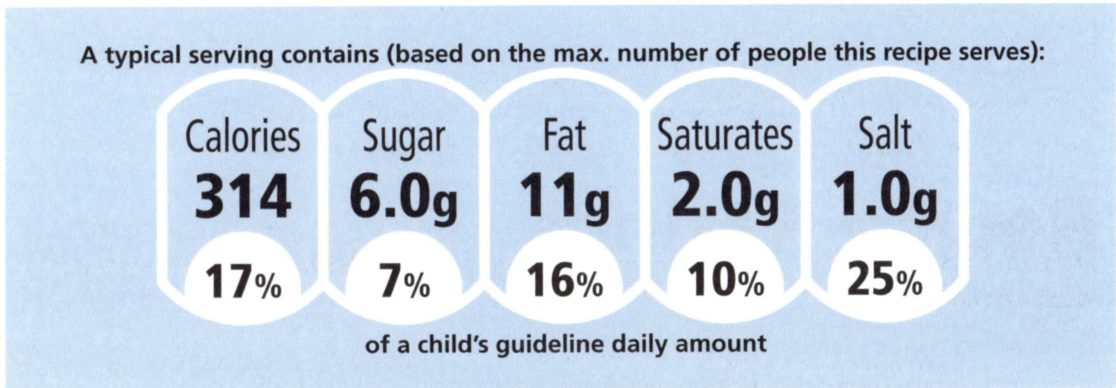

For more information visit our website at www.watchitdoit.com

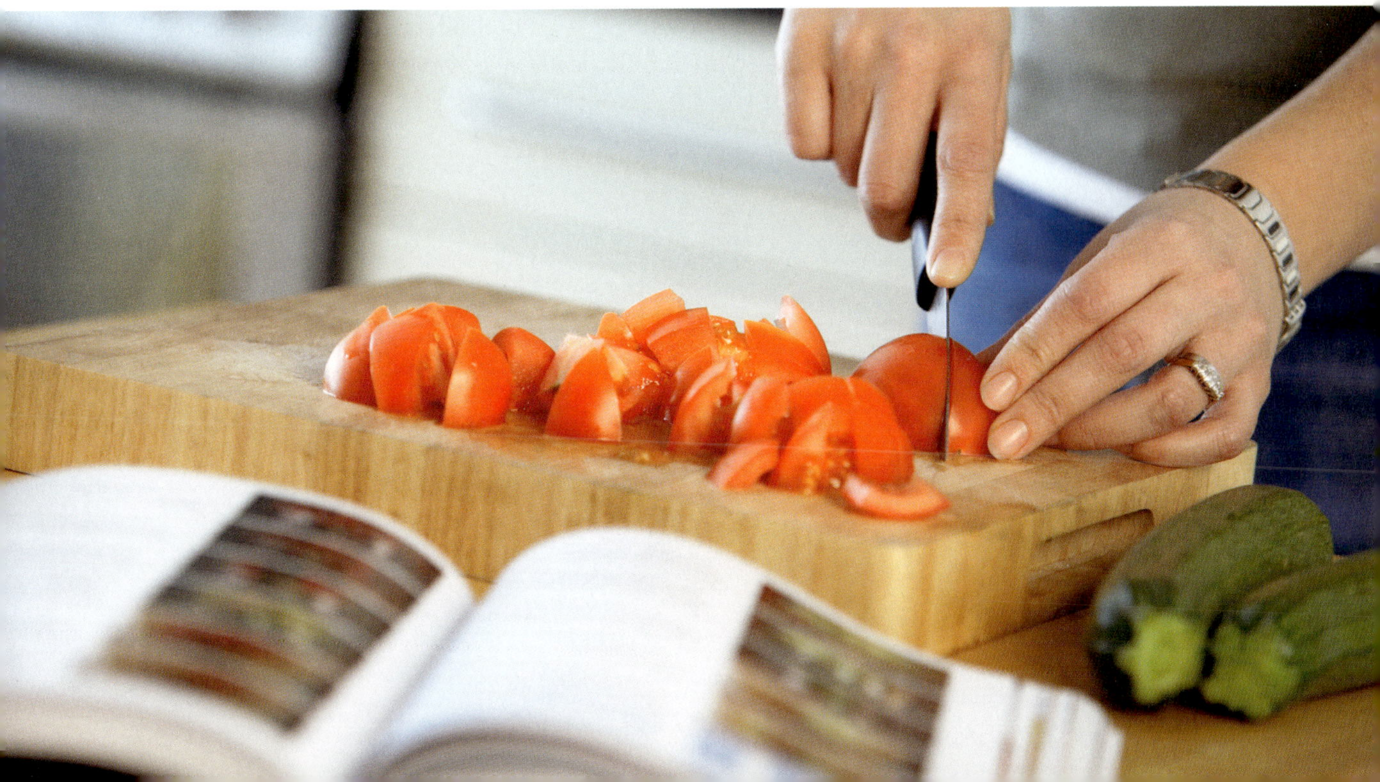

Basic Hygiene & Safety

Please remember that our DVD video does not show our chef undertaking basic hygiene in between cooking and preparation. You must make sure that you take care of this yourself during the recipes, making sure to use clean knives, pots, chopping boards etc.

Take extra care when preparing raw meats and fish to clean your knives and chopping boards. You must also take care to protect yourself at all times when handling hot items or cooking with hot food.

Recipe Ratings

To help you choose which recipe you want to cook, we provide the details of how long it takes to prepare, how long it takes to cook, how many people it will serve and how easy it is to make.

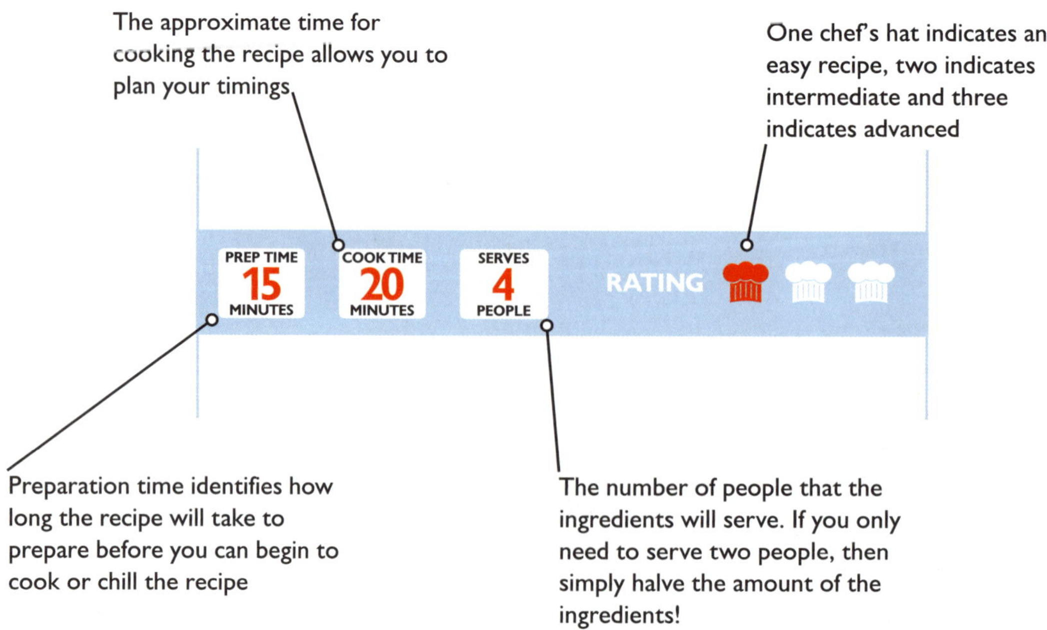

Conversion Tables

To help you make the recipes in *Cooking for Kids Made Easy* we've included a variety of conversion tables below.

Our cooking times are based on using a fan-assisted oven. If you are using a conventional oven increase the temperature by 10°C.

Our timings are provided as guidelines only as individual ovens vary.

OVEN TEMPS.		
110°C	225°F	gas mark ¼
120°C	250°F	gas mark ½
140°C	275°F	gas mark 1
150°C	300°F	gas mark 2
160°C	325°F	gas mark 3
180°C	350°F	gas mark 4
190°C	375°F	gas mark 5
200°C	400°F	gas mark 6
220°C	425°F	gas mark 7
230°C	450°F	gas mark 8
240°C	475°F	gas mark 9

VOLUMES	
2 fl oz	55 ml
3 fl oz	75 ml
5 fl oz	150 ml
10 fl oz	275 ml
1 pint	570 ml
1 ¼ pints	725 ml
1 ¾ pints	1 litre
2 pints	1.2 litres
2 ½ pints	1.5 litres
4 pints	2.25 litres

WEIGHTS	
½ oz	10 g
¾ oz	20 g
1 oz	25 g
1 ½ oz	40 g
2 oz	50 g
2 ½ oz	60 g
3 oz	75 g
4 oz	110 g
4 ½ oz	125 g
5 oz	150 g
6 oz	175 g
7 oz	200 g
8 oz	225 g
9 oz	250 g
10 oz	275 g
12 oz	350 g
1 lb.	450 g
1 lb. 8 oz	700 g
2 lbs.	900 g
3	1.35 kg

SPOON MEASURES	
¼ teaspoon	1.5 ml
½ teaspoon	2.5 ml
1 teaspoon	5 ml
1 tablespoon	15 ml

Utensils

1. small knife
2. chopping knife
3. serrated/bread knife
4. carving knife
5. chopping board
6. fork
7. knife (spreading)
8. tablespoon
9. teaspoon
10. chopsticks
11. wooden spoons
12. silicone spatula

13. slotted spoon
14. serving spoon
15. ladle
16. spatula
17. palette knife
18. potato masher
19. step palette knife/spatula
20. whisk
21. pizza cutter
22. peeler

23. measuring jug
24. small jug
25. large jug
26. sieve
27. colander
28. kitchen scissors

29. tongs
30. pastry brush
31. melon baller
32. meat mallet
33. rolling pin
34. cheese grater

35. large mixing bowl
36. medium mixing bowl
37. small mixing bowl
38. small serving bowl
39. small glass bowl

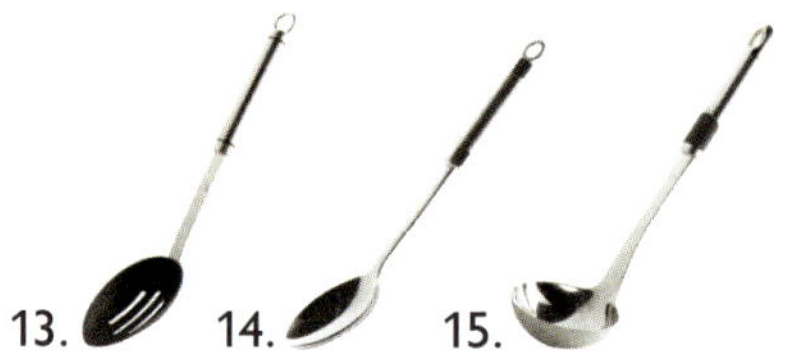

5.
6.
7.
8.
9.
10.
11.
12.
16.
17.
18.
19.
20.
21.
22.
25.
26.
27.
28.
29.
30.
31.
32.
33.
34.
35.
36.
37.
38.
39.

Pots & Pans

1. chargrill pan
2. small frying pan
3. large frying pan
4. frying pan with lid

5. milk pan
6. small saucepan with lid
7. medium saucepan with lid
8. large saucepan with lid/stock pot

1.

5.

Baking & roasting

1–6. roasting/baking trays

7. flat baking tray/silcone-coated flat baking tray
8. pizza tray
9. 18cm-square cake tin
10. 450g loaf tin
11. round cake tin/round cake tin with false base

12. glass oven dish
13. small oven dish
14. large oven dish
15. small oven proof pot

1.

2.

2.
3.
4.
6.
7.
8.

3.
4.
5.
6.
7.
8.
9.
10.
11.
12.
13.
14.
15.

Miscellaneous

1. cling film
2. tin foil
3. baking paper
4. bamboo skewers
5. kitchen blow torch
6. oven gloves
7. oven cloth
8. tea towel

9. espresso cup & saucer
10. egg cup
11. wire rack
12. ramekin dishes
13. tin foil mould
14. tin foil tray

15. ice cream scoop
16. squeezy bottle
17. pudding trays
18. a selection of glasses for serving

19. food processor/blender
20. electric hand-held blender
21. electric hand-held whisk
22. pasta machine
23. metal ring

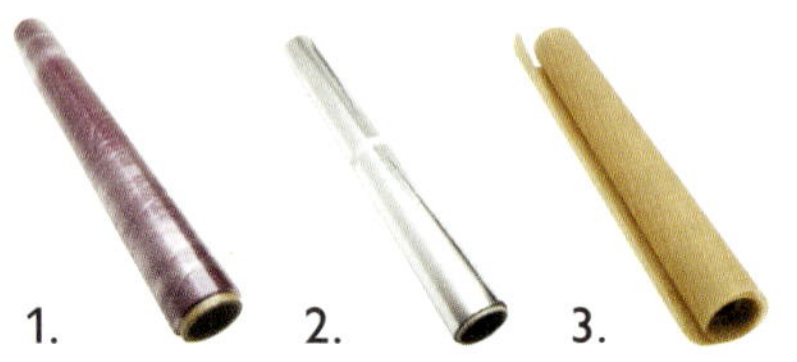
1. 2. 3.

9. 10.

15. 16.

4.
5.
6.
7.
8.
11.
12.
13.
14.
17.
18.
19.
20.
21.
22.
23.

Breakfast

Image taken from video

3 Real Fruit Smoothies

Malted Banana, Strawberry & Raspberry, Fruit Tango

Smoothies are healthy, fun and quick to prepare, which makes them ideal for breakfasts on the run!

PREP TIME 5 MINUTES

RATING

Ingredients

Malted Banana Smoothie
- 3 medium bananas
- 250ml semi-skimmed milk
- 50g malted milk powder
- 1 tablespoon honey
- 8 ice cubes

Strawberry & Raspberry Smoothie
- 200g fresh or frozen raspberries
- 400g fresh or frozen strawberries
- 200ml fresh orange juice

Fruit Tango Smoothie
- 1 medium banana
- 1 peach
- 200g fresh or frozen strawberries
- 1 medium mango
- 200ml fresh orange juice
- 1 tablespoon of runny honey

Utensils

- chopping knife
- chopping board
- large mixing bowl
- tablespoon
- blender
- cloth/tea towel
- straws

A typical serving contains (based on the max. number of people this recipe serves):

Calories	Sugar	Fat	Saturates	Salt
99	19g	1.5g	0.6g	0.1g
6%	22%	2%	3%	2.5%

of a child's guideline daily amount

Malted Banana Smoothie

Prepare the bananas

- Peel the bananas
- Remove any black bits
- Break the bananas up and put them in the blender – there is no need to chop them

Add the ingredients to the blender

- Add all the other ingredients to the blender
- You can use soya milk instead of cows' milk, if you prefer
- The ice cubes are optional

Blend

- Make sure the lid is on tightly
- Put a cloth on top of the blender when you first start it (this will stop any mix from splashing out)
- Blend for about 2 minutes

Serve

- The smoothies should be smooth, foamy and thick
- Enjoy!

Strawberry & Raspberry Smoothie

Prepare the strawberries

- You will need to wash the strawberries before you start
- Cut the tops off
- Halve any large ones

Add the ingredients

- Put the strawberries and the raspberries in the blender with the orange juice

Blend

- Blend for about a minute

Serve

- It should be a smooth and thick consistency
- It's as easy as that!

Fruit Tango Smoothie

Peel and prepare the banana

- Peel the banana and remove any black bits
- Break into chunks

Prepare the peach

- To prepare the peach, cut around the centre stone and twist the 2 halves to separate
- Cut around the stone to remove it
- Roughly chop the peach

Prepare the strawberries

- Wash the strawberries
- Slice the tops off
- Halve any large ones

Peel the mango

- Use as ripe a mango as possible
- The mango is quite tricky to peel, so be careful!
- Peel the skin from the mango, like peeling a potato

Chop the mango

- The mango has a big stone in the centre – put your hand on top of the mango and cut the flesh away from around the stone
- Trim any other flesh from the stone
- Roughly chop the mango flesh

Add and blend

- Put all the fruit in the blender
- Pour in the orange juice
- Finally, spoon in the honey
- Put a cloth on the top and blend for around a minute until smooth and thick

Serve

- Serve and enjoy!
- You can add some more fresh fruit to the top for decoration

image taken from video

Boiled Eggs
with Cheese and Ham Soldiers

A tasty twist on the classic kids' favourite, with ham and cheddar cheese soldiers for dipping.

SERVES 4 PEOPLE

Ingredients

- 4 free-range eggs
- 4 slices bread
- 150g mature cheddar cheese (grated)
- 4 slices of ham

Utensils

- medium saucepan
- toaster
- oven grill tray
- cheese grater
- slotted spoon
- tea towel
- chopping knife
- chopping board
- 4 egg cups

A typical serving contains (based on the max. number of people this recipe serves):

Calories	Sugar	Fat	Saturates	Salt
324	1.0g	20g	10g	1.8g
18%	1.2%	28%	50%	45%

of a child's guideline daily amount

Step 1 Cook

Put the eggs in a pan of cold water

- Put the eggs in a saucepan of cold water – if you put them straight into boiling water they could crack
- Bring the pan to the boil on a high heat

Make the toast

- While the eggs are coming to the boil, lightly toast the bread in a toaster
- Granary bread is a good and healthy option

Turn the heat down

- Once the pan is boiling, turn the heat down to low and simmer for 3 minutes (if you want soft yolks) or 6 minutes (if you want hard yolks)

Put the toast on the grill

- Lay the bread on the grill tray
- Leave the crusts on for the moment – you will cut them off later

Add the toppings

- Sprinkle a little of the cheese onto the toast – this will stop the ham sliding off when dipping!
- Lay 4 slices of ham on top of the cheese
- Sprinkle the rest of the cheese on the top

Put the toast under the grill

- Put the toast under a hot grill for 3–4 minutes

Serve

Remove the eggs from the saucepan

- After the eggs have cooked, carefully remove them from the saucepan with a slotted spoon
- Turn off the heat
- Wrap the eggs in a tea towel to keep them warm

Remove the toast from the grill

- When the cheese is golden and bubbling, remove the toast from the grill

Cut into soldiers

- Cut the toast into soldiers, trimming the crust from either end

Serve

- Cut the top off the egg with a knife and serve with the cheese and ham soldiers

image taken from video

Supreme Scrambled Eggs

Creamy scrambled eggs served on a hot toasted muffin.

PREP TIME	COOK TIME	SERVES
5–10 MINUTES	5 MINUTES	4 PEOPLE

RATING   

Ingredients

- 6 eggs
- 125ml semi-skimmed milk
- parsley, for serving
- 30g butter (plus extra for the toasted muffins)
- 4 English muffins
- salt and pepper

Utensils

- medium mixing bowl
- whisk
- medium saucepan
- wooden spoon
- chopping board
- serrated knife
- spreading knife

A typical serving contains (based on the max. number of people this recipe serves):

Calories	Sugar	Fat	Saturates	Salt
353	4.0g	20g	8.0g	1.1g
20%	5%	28%	40%	27%

of a child's guideline daily amount

Prepare the egg mix

Crack the eggs into a bowl

- Crack the eggs into a large mixing bowl
- Make sure there is no shell in the mix

Add the milk

- Add the milk to the eggs

Season

- Season with a little salt and pepper

Whisk

- Whisk together well

It should be combined

- Whisk until thoroughly combined

Cook the eggs

Put the butter in a pan

- Put a saucepan on a medium heat and add the butter

Add the eggs

- When the butter is sizzling, add all the egg mixture

Stir

- Continually stir the eggs – make sure that the pan doesn't get too hot and burn the eggs
- Take the saucepan off the heat if it's cooking too quickly

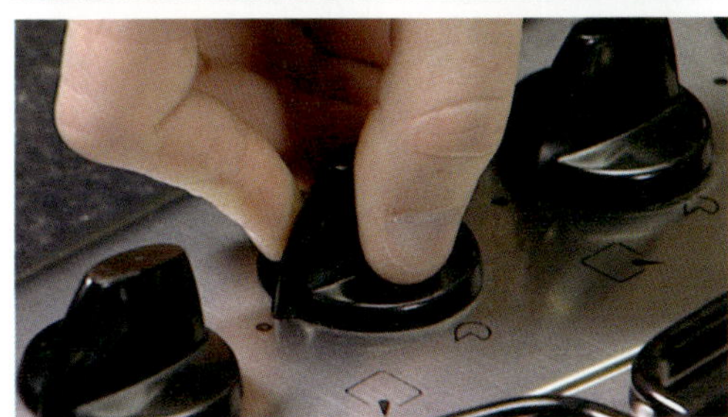

Turn off the heat

- When the eggs begin to thicken up, turn off the heat

Continue to stir

- Keep stirring the eggs, off the heat, until you have the desired consistency

Creamy consistency

- They should be creamy and not too dry

Step 3 Toast the muffins & serve

Put the muffins under the grill

- Split the muffins in two
- Put them under a medium grill until browned

Remove when golden

- When golden, remove from the grill

Butter the muffins

- Butter all of the muffins

Add the egg and garnish

- Top the toasted muffins with the scrambled egg
- Finish with a sprig of parsley and serve

image taken from video

Poached Eggs

This clever way of poaching eggs will be great fun and guarantee you the perfect poached egg every time!

PREP TIME **5** MINUTES

COOK TIME **5–10** MINUTES

SERVES **4** PEOPLE

RATING   

Ingredients

- 4 eggs
- 10ml white wine vinegar
- 4 thick slices bread
- butter (for the toast)
- a little flat leaf parsley (for decoration)

Utensils

- medium or small saucepan
- small bowl or jug
- whisk
- toaster
- spreading knife
- chopping board
- metal ring
- slotted spoon
- cloth

A typical serving contains (based on the max. number of people this recipe serves):

Calories	Sugar	Fat	Saturates	Salt
233	1.0g	11g	4.0g	0.9g
13%	1.2%	16%	20%	45%

of a child's guideline daily amount

Step 1 Cook the eggs

Bring a pan of water to the boil

- Bring a half-filled small or medium saucepan of water to the boil

Crack the egg into a bowl

- Crack the egg into a small bowl – this will make it easier to drop into the water

Add the white wine vinegar

- When the water is boiling, add the white wine vinegar

Whisk the water

- Using a whisk, thoroughly whisk the water in a circular motion – it has to be moving quite fast before you can drop the egg in

Add the egg

- Carefully drop the first egg into the centre of the water – you can only cook one egg at a time
- Turn the heat down to simmer
- Cook for 3 minutes for soft yolks or 6 minutes for hard yolks

Step 2 Make the toast & serve

Toast

- Lightly toast the bread

Butter and cut

- Butter the toast before cutting as it is easier
- Then use a 10cm metal ring to cut a circle from each piece and put the circles of toast on a plate
- You could also cut the toast into triangles

Remove the egg

- When it's cooked, remove the egg with a slotted spoon

Drain the egg

- Put the egg onto a clean, dry cloth to drain and add the next egg to the water (the water will need to be whisked again before adding the egg)

Serve

- When they are ready, put the poached eggs on top of the toast and finish with a sprig of parsley

image taken from video

Full English Breakfast

This recipe simplifies and cuts down the amount of work usually needed for an English breakfast. Cooking on a grilling rack will reduce the amount of fat normally found in an English breakfast.

Ingredients

- 4 flat mushrooms
- 2 tomatoes
- 4 good-quality sausages or chipolatas
- 4 rindless bacon rashers
- 100ml vegetable oil
- salt and pepper
- a little sugar
- a little butter, softened
- 4 eggs

Utensils

- chopping board
- small knife
- small bowl
- grill tray
- 4 ramekin dishes or small oven dishes
- baking tray
- oven gloves
- tongs

A typical serving contains (based on the max. number of people this recipe serves):

Calories	Sugar	Fat	Saturates	Salt
362	2.0g	32g	8.0g	1.7g
20%	2%	46%	50%	42%

of a child's guideline daily amount

Step 1 Preparation

Peel the mushrooms

- Peel the mushrooms using a small knife and remove the stalks

Cut the tomatoes

- Remove the green stalks from the tomatoes and then halve them

Place everything on a grill tray

- Place the mushrooms, tomatoes, sausages and bacon on the grill tray

Drizzle with oil

- Drizzle the mushrooms and tomatoes with a little oil, to keep them moist while cooking

Season with salt and pepper

- Season the tomatoes and mushrooms with salt and pepper
- You can also put a little sugar on the tomatoes to sweeten them

Put in a pre-heated oven

- Put the grill tray in an oven, pre-heated to 180°C (350°F or gas mark 4) for 10–15 minutes

Step 2 Bake the eggs

Butter the ramekin dishes

- Rub a little softened butter inside each of the 4 ramekins or small oven dishes
- It's easier to take the dishes in and out of the oven if they are on a baking tray

Put the ramekin dishes in the oven

- Heat the ramekin dishes in the oven with the breakfast for 2 minutes

Take them out of the oven

- After 2 minutes, remove the dishes from the oven using an oven glove

Add the eggs to the ramekin dishes

- Crack 1 egg into each dish

Put the eggs back into the oven

- Cook the eggs in the oven for 10–12 minutes

Step 3 Serve

Remove from the oven

- Remove the grill tray from the oven
- Remove the baking tray from the oven using an oven glove

Place egg ramekin on a plate

- Using an oven glove, place an egg ramekin dish on a plate to serve
- Tell your kids to be careful – the ramkin dishes are hot!

Dress the plate

- Plate 1 sausage, ½ a tomato, a mushroom and 1 slice of bacon

Serve and enjoy!

image taken from video

Porridge Plus

with 3 Great Toppings

A classic, healthy, home-made breakfast – we have given you some suggestions to make it more exciting. Strawberries and brown sugar, apricots and almonds, bananas and hazelnuts – a great slow release of energy to start the day!

PREP TIME 10 MINUTES

COOK TIME 8 MINUTES

SERVES 4 PEOPLE

RATING

Ingredients

Porridge

- 1 litre water
- 250g rolled oats
- pinch of salt (optional)
- 50ml milk (semi-skimmed)

1 - Brown sugar and strawberry

- 100g fresh strawberries
- 50g brown sugar

2 – Apricot and toasted, flaked almonds

- 50g flaked almonds
- 100g fresh or dried apricots
- 50ml honey

3 – Banana and hazelnut

- 50g hazelnuts
- 100g or 1 medium banana
- 50g muscovado sugar

Utensils

- medium saucepan
- large jug
- wooden spoon
- chopping board
- small knife
- large serving spoon
- teaspoon

A typical serving contains (based on the max. number of people this recipe serves):

Calories	Sugar	Fat	Saturates	Salt
413	20g	13.5g	0.7g	trace
23%	24%	19%	3.5%	<1%

of a child's guideline daily amount

Make the porridge

Pour the water and oats in the pan

- Put the cold water and porridge oats into a large saucepan and cook on a medium heat

Stir thoroughly

- Stir the porridge continuously with a wooden spoon to stop it sticking to the bottom of the pan

Bring it to the boil and simmer

- Bring it to the boil, then lower the heat and simmer for 4 minutes

Check the consistency

- When the porridge is thick and creamy it is ready
- You can add a little more water to get your desired consistency

When it's ready, turn off the heat

- You can add a pinch of salt for flavour if you like

Strawberry topping

Chop the strawberries

- Remove the tops of the strawberries and slice them into quarters

Spoon the porridge into bowls

- Serve the porridge in bowls and pour a little milk on the top

Add some strawberries

- Sprinkle strawberries onto the porridge

Add some sugar

- Sprinkle some brown or muscavado sugar on the top

Serve

Apricot & almond topping

Chop the apricots

- Chop the dried apricots into small pieces

Spoon the porridge into bowls

- Serve the porridge in bowls and pour a little milk on top

Add some apricots and almonds

- Sprinkle on apricot and almonds

Drizzle the honey on top

- Drizzle honey on the top to taste

Serve

Banana & hazelnut topping

Peel and chop the banana

- Remove any bruised banana

Spoon the porridge into bowls

- Serve the porridge in bowls and pour a little milk on top

Add some banana and hazelnuts

- Add some banana
- Add a few hazelnuts

Sprinkle on some brown sugar

- Sprinkle some brown or muscavado sugar on the top

Serve

Image taken from video

Home-Roasted Cereal

with 3 Great Toppings

This great home-made cereal mix can be made in larger amounts and then stored in the fridge for up to 3 months. Packed with fruit and nuts, try it topped with Greek yoghurt and honey, crème fraîche and blueberry or orange and chocolate milk!

MAKES 8–12 PORTIONS

RATING

Ingredients

- 400g rolled oats
- 50g dried apricots
- 30g dried apples
- 30g Pecans
- 1 teaspoon ground cinnamon
- 35g flaked coconut
- 20g malted milk powder
- 30g sunflower seeds
- 30g pumpkin seeds
- 30g hazelnuts
- 1 tablespoon vegetable oil
- 120g honey (runny)
- 55g sultanas
- 40g craisins (sweetened dried cranberries)

Greek yoghurt and honey
- 150ml low-fat Greek yoghurt
- 50ml Acacia honey

Blueberries and crème fraîche
- 150ml crème fraîche
- 50g blueberries

Orange segments and chocolate milk
- 50g chocolate powder or drinking chocolate
- 500ml semi-skimmed milk
- 2 medium oranges, peeled and segmented

Utensils

- large roasting tray
- small chopping knife
- chopping board
- oven gloves
- wooden spoon
- large mixing bowl

A typical serving contains (based on the max. number of people this recipe serves):

Calories	Sugar	Fat	Saturates	Salt
323	23g	13g	3.0g	0.1g
18%	27%	19%	15%	2%

of a child's guideline daily amount

Make the cereal

Sprinkle the oats onto a baking tray

- Sprinkle the oats onto a baking tray

Bake them in the oven

- Roast the oats on the top shelf of an oven pre-heated at 200°C (400°F or gas mark 6) for 5 minutes
- While they are roasting, prepare the fruit and pecans

Chop the apricots into small pieces

- Chop the apricots into small pieces

Chop the apples into small pieces

- Chop the apples into small pieces

Chop the pecan nuts roughly

- Chop the pecan nuts roughly

After 5 minutes, remove from oven

- After 5 minutes, remove the roasted oats from the oven
- Leave the oven on

Add more ingredients

- Sprinkle the cinnamon over the the oats
- Add the coconut
- Add the malted milk powder
- Add the sunflower and pumpkin seeds
- Add the hazelnuts and pecans

Add the vegetable oil and honey

- Mix thoroughly before adding the oil and honey
- Pour the vegetable oil over the oats
- Pour the honey over the oats
- Mix thoroughly again

Put the cereal back in the oven

- Put the cereal back in the oven for 5 more minutes, uncovered

Remove it from the oven

- Remove the cereal from the oven after 5 minutes and mix it together thoroughly

Roast it for another 5 minutes

- Roast the cereal once again for 5 more minutes to finish

Add the fruit

- Remove the fruit from the oven
- Add the dried apricots, dried apples, sultanas and craisins
- Mix well
- Turn off the oven

Store in a plastic container

- You can store the mixture in a plastic container once it has cooled down

Greek yoghurt & honey

Greek topping

- Spoon the cereal into a bowl
- Add a dollop of Greek yoghurt
- Drizzle honey on top
- Serve

Crème fraîche & blueberry

Crème fraîche and blueberry

- Spoon the cereal into a bowl
- Add a dollop of crème fraîche
- Sprinkle the blueberries on the top
- Serve

Chocolate & orange topping

Chocolate and orange

- Add the cocoa to the milk and then whisk together thoroughly

Peel the orange

- First, cut the top and bottom off the orange
- Then cut the remaining skin off like this

Cut into segments and squeeze

- Cut the orange segments out like this
- Hold the orange in your hand and cut each segment out as shown in the DVD video for this recipe – make sure you discard the white membrane

Remove the pips

- Make sure you remove all of the pips from the orange segments

Serve

- Spoon the cereal into a bowl
- Place some orange segments on top and pour over the chocolate milk
- Now serve!

image taken from video

Breakfast Muffins and Crumpets

Muffins and crumpets are great topped with a whole range of sweet and savoury ingredients; brie, bacon and tomato, mixed berries and yoghurt and peanut butter with banana.

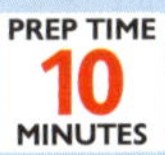

Ingredients

- 2 English muffins or 4 crumpets

Peanut butter and banana
- 1 medium banana
- 50g honey
- 150g peanut butter

Brie, bacon and tomato
- 100g brie
- 2 large plum tomatoes
- 4 slices of rindless bacon

Mixed berry and natural yoghurt
- 250g mixed berries (raspberries, blueberries, blackberries, strawberries, loganberries)
- 100g raspberry jam
- 100ml natural yoghurt

Utensils

- small chopping knife
- chopping board
- grill tray
- teaspoons
- serrated knife
- toaster
- tongs
- spatula

A typical serving contains (based on the max. number of people this recipe serves):

Calories	Sugar	Fat	Saturates	Salt
240	20g	11g	4.0g	0.9g
13%	17%	16%	20%	22%

of a child's guideline daily amount

Peanut butter & banana

Peel the banana

- Peel the banana

Chop the banana

- Chop the banana into slices

Toast the crumpets

- Toast the crumpets lightly under the grill

Spread the peanut butter

- Spread the peanut butter on the crumpets

Add the banana

- Top the crumpets with the slices of banana

Drizzle with honey

- Finally, drizzle with honey and serve!

Brie, bacon & tomato

Chop the brie into thin slices

- Chop the brie into thin slices

Chop the tomatoes into slices

- Chop the tomatoes into slices

Grill the bacon

- Grill the bacon lightly under a medium grill until 'lighty grilled' because we will cook the bacon again later

Halve the muffins and toast them

- Cut the muffins in half and toast them

Add the brie to the muffins

- Place the muffins on the grill tray
- Put a slice of brie on top of each muffin half

Add the bacon to the top

- Put some bacon on top

Add the tomato

- Put 2 slices of tomato on top of the bacon

Add more brie to the top

- Put more brie on top of each slice of tomato

Put the muffins back under the grill

- Place the muffins under the grill for 3–4 minutes to melt the brie and finish the bacon

Serve

- Serve and enjoy!

Mixed berry

Chop the strawberries

- Cut the stalks off the strawberries
- Then cut them in half

Toast the crumpets

- Toast the crumpets under the grill

Coat with the jam

- Remove the crumpets from the grill
- Spread the jam on top of them

Add the berries

- Add some strawberries, raspberries, blackberries and loganberries as required

Top with yoghurt and serve

- Put a dollop of yoghurt on top of the berries
- Serve

Image taken from video

Sweet French Toast

Crispy on the outside and gooey in the middle – wonderfully finished with cinnamon, sugar and maple syrup.

PREP TIME **10** MINUTES

COOK TIME **15** MINUTES

SERVES **4** PEOPLE

RATING   

Ingredients

- 4 thick slices white bread
- 1 egg
- 2 tablespoons caster sugar
- 1 tablespoon semi-skimmed milk
- 30g butter
- ¼ teaspoon ground cinnamon to serve
- 2 tablespoons caster sugar to serve
- maple syrup to serve

Utensils

- 9cm biscuit cutter/metal ring
- 2 medium mixing bowls
- fork or whisk
- large frying pan
- spatula
- palette knife
- kitchen towels or clean tea towel
- tablespoon

A typical serving contains (based on the max. number of people this recipe serves):

Calories	Sugar	Fat	Saturates	Salt
203	9.0g	9.0g	4.5g	0.7g
11%	10%	13%	22%	18%

of a child's guideline daily amount

Prepare & make the mix

Cut circles from the bread

- Cut circles from the bread using the biscuit cutter

Crack an egg into a bowl

- Crack an egg into a bowl

Add the caster sugar

- Add the 2 tablespoons of caster sugar to the egg

Add the milk

- Add the milk

Whisk

- Whisk the egg, sugar and milk together until it becomes combined and smooth in texture, like this

Cook and serve

Add 30g of butter to the pan

- Add the butter to a pan on a medium heat
- Allow it to melt

Dip the bread in the egg mix

- When the butter is foaming, dip the bread into the egg mix
- Allow the bread to drain before putting it in the pan

Add the dipped bread to the pan

- Put the eggy bread in the frying pan

Turn it over when it's brown

- Cook the bread in the butter for 2–3 minutes until it's browned on the bottom
- Check the bread by lifting it to see if it is ready to turn over

Cook on other side

- Cook the other side of the bread until that has browned too

Drain it on a tea towel

- When it's ready, remove the bread from the pan and drain it on a tea towel or kitchen roll to remove any excess butter
- Turn off the heat

Place the toast on a plate

- Place the toast on a plate, ready to serve

Mix the cinnamon and sugar

- Put the cinnamon and sugar in a bowl and mix them together using a spoon

Sprinkle them over the toast

- Sprinkle the cinnamon and sugar over the toast

Drizzle with some maple syrup

- Drizzle some maple syrup over the toast to finish

It's ready to serve

- Serve and enjoy!

Image taken from video

Savoury French Toast

Savoury French toast can be just as tasty as sweet. This simple, tasty breakfast dish is given an extra twist by the sweet cherry tomatoes.

PREP TIME 5 MINUTES 
COOK TIME 15 MINUTES 
SERVES 4 PEOPLE 

RATING   

Ingredients

- 2 eggs
- 3 tablespoons semi-skimmed milk
- salt and pepper
- 4 thick slices white bread
- 12 cherry tomatoes
- 50ml olive oil
- 30g butter

Utensils

- bowl
- fork or whisk
- serrated knife
- chopping board
- grill tray/baking tray
- small frying pan
- spatula
- palette knife
- kitchen towels or clean tea towel
- tongs

A typical serving contains (based on the max. number of people this recipe serves):

Calories	Sugar	Fat	Saturates	Salt
287	2.5g	20g	6.0g	0.8g
16%	3%	28%	30%	20%

of a child's guideline daily amount

Make the mix & prepare

Crack the eggs into a bowl

- Crack the eggs into a bowl

Whisk the eggs

- Whisk the eggs until they are smooth

Add the milk

- Add the milk

Add the salt and pepper

- Add the salt and pepper

Whisk again

- Whisk the mix again thoroughly

Cut the crusts off the bread

- Cut the crusts off the bread

Cut it into triangles

- Cut the bread into triangles

Cook and serve

Put the tomatoes on a baking tray

- Place the cherry tomatoes on a baking tray

Drizzle with olive oil and season

- Drizzle them with olive oil and season with salt and pepper

Put them under the grill

- Put the cherry tomatoes under a medium grill for 5–6 minutes

Add the oil and butter to a pan

- Place a pan on a medium heat
- Add the oil to the pan
- Add the butter to the pan

Dip the bread in the egg and fry

- Dip the bread in the egg mixture, allow it to drain then place in the pan
- Cook for 2–3 minutes

When it's brown, turn over

- When it's browned on the underside, turn it over
- Then cook the other side for 2–3 minutes

Remove when brown both sides

- When both sides are brown, remove the toast and drain it on a tea towel or some kitchen roll
- Turn off the heat

Transfer to plate ready to serve

- Transfer the toast to a plate ready to serve

Add the cherry tomatoes and serve

- After 5–6 minutes remove the tomatoes from the grill
- Put the cherry tomatoes on the plate
- Remember to turn off the grill

image taken from video

Welsh Rarebit

The original cheese on toast! Always a favourite with the kids, but be careful not to add too much mustard! You can also make Buck Rarebit – just add a poached egg on top at the end!

PREP TIME **10** MINUTES | COOK TIME **15** MINUTES | SERVES **4** PEOPLE

RATING   

Ingredients

- 5 slices thick white bread (4 for toasting, 1 to make breadcrumbs)
- 40ml semi-skimmed milk
- 175g mature cheddar cheese (freshly grated – not ready-grated)
- 12g plain flour
- ½ tablespoon English mustard
- 2 egg yolks
- salt and pepper
- Worcester sauce to taste
- parsley for decoration

Utensils

- serrated knife
- chopping board
- food processor or hand-held blender
- small or medium non-stick saucepan
- cheese grater
- wooden spoon
- silicon spatula/spoon
- knife or palette knife for spreading

A typical serving contains (based on the max. number of people this recipe serves):

Calories	Sugar	Fat	Saturates	Salt
388	2.0g	18g	10.6g	1.4g
21%	2%	26%	52%	35%

of a child's guideline daily amount

Make the breadcrumbs

Prepare the bread

- Chop the crusts off the slice of bread
- Slice it into strips

Put bread into processor and blend

- Add the bread to the processor and blend until it becomes fine breadcrumbs

The breadcrumbs should be fine

- Blend until the breadcrumbs are as fine as possible

Step 2

Make the Welsh Rarebit

Melt the cheese into the milk

- Place a saucepan on a low or medium heat so you can melt the cheese into the milk
- Add the milk to the saucepan
- Add the grated cheese to the saucepan

Keep stirring!

- Stir the cheese contiuously – don't let it boil as this will split the cheese
- When all the cheese is melted, it's ready
- When it starts to peel away from the sides, take the pan off the heat

Add the flour and breadcrumbs

- Add the plain flour to the pan
- Add the breadcrumbs to the pan

Add the mustard

- Now add the mustard to the pan

Mix together thoroughly

- Mix everything together thoroughly until it forms a ball shape – when this happens it's ready

Separate the egg yolks

- Seperate the egg yolks and discard the egg whites

Add the yolks

- Add the yolks to the pan

Mix together thoroughly

- Mix everything together with a wooden spoon

Season and mix

- Season with salt and pepper
- Then mix together well

Put the Rarebit mix in a small bowl

- You can keep the Rarebit mix in the fridge and use it later if you like as it will last 2–3 days

Serve

Toast the bread

- Toast the bread under a medium grill for 2–5 minutes

Spread the Rarebit on the toast

- Spread the Rarebit on the toast

Drizzle on a little Worcester sauce

- Add a splash of Worcester sauce if you like!

Lower the grill rack

- Lower the grill rack

Put the Rarebit under the grill

- Put the Rarebit under the grill

Remove it when it's lightly browned

- Remove the Rarebit from the grill when it becomes lightly browned

Remove crusts, cut into triangles

- Remove the crusts
- Cut the Rarebit into triangles

Serve

- Add a little parsley for decoration
- Serve

Tea Time

Teatime

Image taken from video

Home-Made Fish Fingers

with Peas and Home-Made Tartar Sauce

Pure 100% fresh fish coated in fresh breadcrumbs, served with peas and a piquant home-made tartar sauce.

PREP TIME	COOK TIME	SERVES
15 MINUTES	10 MINUTES	4 PEOPLE

RATING  

Ingredients

- 4 slices bread (to make 200g breacrumbs)
- 400g fresh cod (about 2 medium fillets)
- 2 eggs
- 100g plain flour
- 100ml sunflower oil
- 200g garden peas
- salt and pepper
- 1 lemon

For the tartar sauce

- 1 lemon (zest and juice)
- 100g mayonnaise
- 30g gherkins
- 30g capers

Utensils

- chopping knife
- chopping board
- food processor (to make the breadcrumbs)
- 2 large mixing bowls
- fish knife (for filleting – optional)
- small mixing bowl
- fork
- cheese grater
- silicon spatula/spoon
- frying pan
- medium saucepan
- palette knife
- spatula
- kitchen roll
- tablespoon

A typical serving contains (based on the max. number of people this recipe serves):

Calories	Sugar	Fat	Saturates	Salt
664	3.0g	34g	5.0g	1.9g
37%	3%	48%	25%	47%

of a child's guideline daily amount

Make the breadcrumbs

Prepare the bread

- You can buy dried breadcrumbs, but not fresh
- To make 200g of breadcrumbs you will need about 4 slices
- Remove the crusts from the bread
- Cut the bread into chunks

Add to the food processor

- Add the chunks of bread to the food processor

Turn on the food processor

- Use the food processor for about 20 seconds to make the breadcrumbs

Pour the breadcrumbs into a bowl

- Put the breadcrumbs in a large mixing bowl and keep them to one side until you need them

Prepare the fish

Skin the fish

- To skin the fish, put it on the chopping board, skin side down and, holding the skin, cut the flesh away

Cut out the bones

- Cut off the thick part of the cod and check along the length for any bones as this is where they will be
- Check you have removed all bones

Cut the fish into fingers

- Once you have removed all the bones, cut the fish into chunky fingers

Coat the fish

Crack the eggs into a bowl

- Put the flour in a large mixing bowl
- Lay out the flour, eggs and breadcrumb bowls next to each other
- Crack the eggs into a small mixing bowl

Beat the eggs

- Beat the eggs with a fork

Season the eggs and the flour

- Season the eggs and the flour with salt and pepper

Coat all the fish with flour

- Drop the fish into the flour and completely cover it using your left hand

Drop it into the egg

- Then put the coated fish into the egg

Coat the fish in egg

- Completely cover the fish in egg
- Again use only your left hand and keep your right hand dry

Drop it into the breadcrumbs

- Then drop the fish into the breadcrumbs, but don't get breadcrumbs on your left hand

Coat the fish in breadcrumbs

- Shake the bowl and coat the fish in the breadcrumbs using your right hand
- Then put the fish on a clean plate ready for cooking
- Don't pile the fish fingers on top of each other as they will stick together

Make the tartar sauce

Grate the lemon

- Grate the zest from the lemon

Put in a bowl with the mayonnaise

- Put the zest in a bowl with the mayonnaise

Cut the lemon in half

- Halve the lemon

Squeeze the juice into a bowl

- Squeeze the juice from half the lemon into the bowl through a sieve to catch any pips
- Use a fork to help you do this

Mix everything together

- Mix the lemon zest, juice and mayonnaise together

Dice the gherkins

- Chop the gherkins into fine strips, then dice them into very small pieces
- You can also use a food processor for this
- Add them to the bowl

Chop the capers finely

- Chop the capers finely
- Add the capers to the bowl

Mix together thoroughly

- Mix them together thoroughly with a spoon or spatula

Season

- Season with salt and pepper

Mix again

- Mix again and that's it!

Cook the fish & peas

Put a pan of water on to boil

- Bring a pan of water to the boil

Add oil to the frying pan

- Put a frying pan on a medium heat and cover the bottom with vegetable oil

Add the fish fingers to the pan

- Add the fish fingers to the pan

Shallow fry them

- Let the fish fingers shallow fry

Add salt to the water when it's boiling

- When the water is boiling, add a pinch of salt

Add peas

- Then add the peas
- The peas will take about 5 minutes to cook

Check and turn them over

- Turn the fish fingers over after a couple of minutes when they begin to turn a golden colour underneath

Remove from the frying pan

- Keep turning the fish fingers occasionally
- When they have browned on both sides and firmed up, they are done – this should take about 5 minutes
- Remove them from the pan, drain them on a kitchen towel and turn off the heat

Drain the peas

- After about 5 minutes, drain the peas

Cut the lemon into wedges

- Cut the lemon into wedges

Remove the pips and core

- Cut away the core from each wedge and remove any pips

Serve

- Serve the fish fingers with the tartar sauce in a small bowl on the plate, a wedge of lemon and the peas

image taken from video

Batterless Fish

and Oven-Baked Chunky Chips

A very light coating of thin, crispy batter and oven-baked chunky chips make this famous dish a healthier alternative.

Ingredients

- 500g potatoes (maris piper)
- pinch of salt
- 1 kg of hake, haddock or cod (appro imatley 4 small fillets skinned and boned)
- 3 tablespoons olive oil
- 50g plain flour
- vegetable oil (for deep fat fryer)
- 100g mayonnaise
- 1 lemon
- parsley for decoration

For the batter
- 120g self-raising flour
- 200ml cold water
- sea salt and pepper

Utensils

- vegetable peeler
- chopping knife
- chopping board
- 3 medium mixing bowls
- medium saucepan
- sieve
- large roasting tray
- whisk
- deep fat fryer
- slotted spoon

A typical serving contains (based on the max. number of people this recipe serves):

Calories	Sugar	Fat	Saturates	Salt
821	2.0g	45g	6.0g	0.8g
46%	2%	64%	30%	4%

of a child's guideline daily amount

Prepare chunky chips & fish

Peel the potatoes

- First, peel the potatoes with a vegetable peeler
- Maris Piper potatoes are good for chips as they absorb less fat than other varieties of potato when cooking

Chop them into chunky chips

- Halve the potatoes and cut them into thick chips
- Chunky chips are healthier than thinner ones as they absorb less fat

Put them in a bowl of water

- Put the chips in a bowl of cold water – this removes some of the starch and stops them sticking together when cooking

Put them in a pan

- Take the chips out of the bowl and put them in a saucepan

Cover them with cold water

- Cover them with cold water

Add salt

- Add a pinch of salt

Put the lid on and boil

- Put the lid on the pan and bring it to the boil
- Once the water has boiled, turn the heat down and simmer the chips for 2 minutes
- This will par-boil them before you finish cooking them in the oven

Remove the skin from the fish

- You can use cod, haddock, hake or any fish you like
- Your fishmonger can skin and bone the fish for you – if not, put it on the chopping board, skin side down and, holding the skin, cut the flesh away

Remove any bones

- Run your fingers along the fish to check for bones
- Cut off the thin part to the side to leave you with a nice chunky fillet of fish
- You may need to cut the fillet into smaller pieces so it will fit in the fryer!

Bake the chips

Check the chips

- After 2 minutes, check the chips to see if they are cooked

Drain the chips

- Drain the chips after 2 minutes' boiling
- Turn off the heat

Put them in a roasting tray

- Put the chips in a large roasting tray

Drizzle with oil and season

- Drizzle them with oil and season with salt and pepper

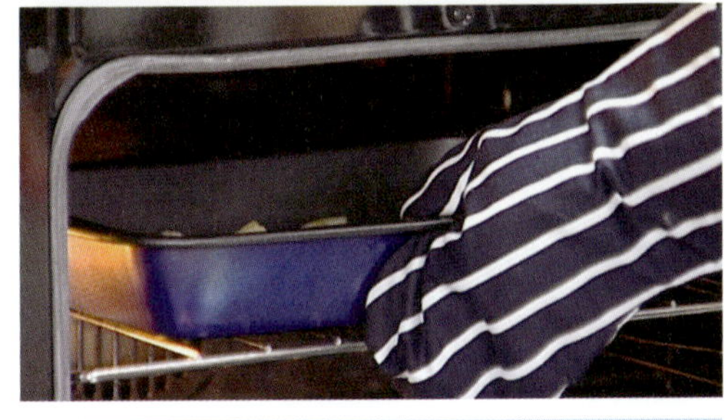

Put into the oven

- Cook the chips in a pre-heated oven at 220°C (425°F or gas mark 7) for 10–15 minutes

Make the batter

Put the flour in a bowl

- Put the flour in a large mixing bowl

Add the water and mix together

- Add the water to the flour
- Whisk together until you have a thick consistency

It should be thick and smooth

- The batter should be thick and smooth

Season with salt and pepper

- Season with sea salt and pepper
- Put to one side

Step 4 Coat the fish & cook

Cover the fish with flour

- Turn the heat in the fryer to 170°C to allow it to warm up while you coat the fish
- Put the fish in the plain flour in a large mixing bowl and completely coat the fish in the flour

Coat the fish in batter

- Then coat the floured fish in the batter

Drain the batter from the fish

- Using your hand, scrape the excess batter off the fish

Put the fish in the deep fat fryer

- Place the fish in the deep fat fryer, laying it away from you
- Be careful the oil is very hot!

Cook until golden brown

- Cook the fish until it's golden brown
- The fish should take about 5–8 minutes, depending on the size

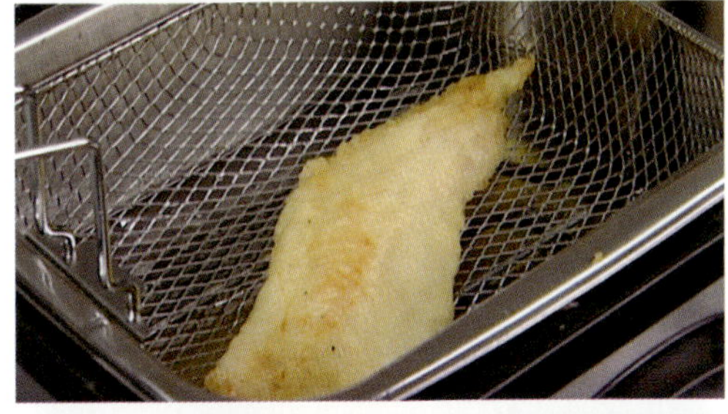

Remove the fish

- When the batter has turned a golden brown, take the fish out of the oil and put it on a kitchen towel to absorb any excess oil
- Turn off the fryer

Remove the chips

- When the chips have browned, take them out of the oven
- Turn off the heat

Serve

- Cut the lemon into wedges
- Serve the fish and chips with a dollop of mayonnaise and a lemon wedge
- Add a sprig of parsley for decoration

image taken from video

Home-Made Beef Burgers

with Home-Made Tomato Sauce

100% pure lean minced beef, nothing added. Served with our home-made tomato sauce and lots of salad. Leave out the cheese for a healthier burger.

PREP TIME 15 MINUTES

COOK TIME 15 MINUTES

SERVES 4 PEOPLE

RATING

Ingredients

For the burgers

- 500g lean minced beef
- salt and pepper
- plain flour for dusting
- 4 slices cheddar cheese
- 4 good-quality sesame baps
- a few iceberg lettuce leaves

For the tomato sauce

- 1 onion
- knob of butter
- tablespoon balsamic vinegar
- ½ a teaspoon caster sugar
- 1 x 400g tin good quality chopped plum tomatoes
- salt and pepper

Utensils

- large mixing bowl
- small frying pan
- spatula
- metal rings
- small chopping knife
- chopping board
- saucepan
- wooden spoon
- food processor
- grill tray
- tongs
- bread knife
- flat baking tray

A typical serving contains (based on the max. number of people this recipe serves):

Calories	Sugar	Fat	Saturates	Salt
545	7.0g	30g	15g	1.5g
30%	8%	43%	75%	47%

of a child's guideline daily amount

Make the burgers

Put the mince in a bowl

- Put the mince in a large mixing bowl

Season

- Season with salt and pepper

Mix together with your hands

- Mix the mince together with your hands

Make a small burger to test

- Before cooking all the burgers, make a small burger from the mix

Cook the test burger

- Cook the test burger, as shown in the DVD, in the small frying pan
- Taste it to check you've got the seasoning right
- Re-season if needed

Flour the work surface

- Sprinkle the flour onto the work surface

Roll the mince and coat in flour

- Roll the mince into a sausage shape, coating it in the flour whilst rolling

Split the mince into 4

- Separate the mince into 4 equal pieces

Flatten the mince into metal rings

- Use the metal rings to form the mince into nice, neat burger shapes
- Put the burgers on a plate to one side until you cook them

Step 2 Make the ketchup

Peel and dice the onion

- To make the tomato sauce, first peel the onion and dice it finely

Put the butter in the saucepan

- Put a saucepan on a medium heat and melt the butter

Add the onion

- When the butter is foaming, add the onion

Fry lightly until translucent

- Fry the onions lightly – we don't want them to go brown, just to turn translucent

Add the balsamic vinegar and sugar

- Add the balsamic vinegar and sugar to the onions

Stir and simmer for 1 minute

- Simmer the sauce for 1 minute

Add the chopped tomatoes

- Add the tin of chopped tomatoes and stir

Simmer

- Stir and simmer the sauce for about 10 minutes
- After 10 minutes turn off the heat and allow to cool
- You can keep the sauce chunky if you want or put it in a food processor to make it smooth

Pick the lettuce leaves

- Meanwhile, pick the leaves from the lettuce

Grill the burgers

Place the burgers on the grill

- Put the burgers on the grill pan

Put them under grill

- Put the grill on to a high heat and put the shelf to the top
- Grill the burgers for about 4–5 minutes each side

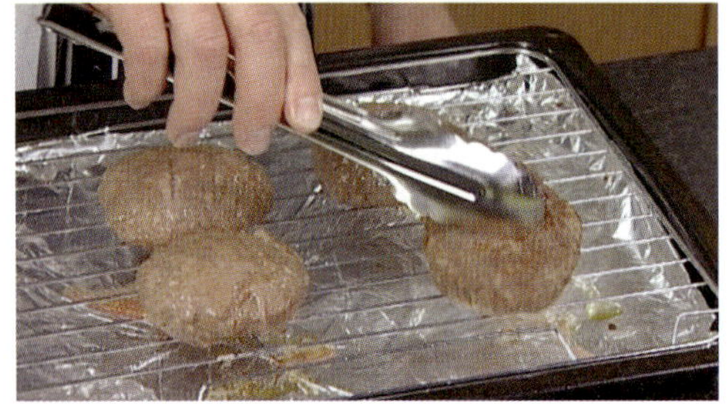

Turn the burgers over

- Keep checking the burgers and turn them halfway through cooking

Put them back under the grill

- Put them back under the grill to finish cooking

Check they're cooked

- Test the burgers are cooked by cutting into one – if the juices are clear, its cooked!

Add cheese

- Put a slice of cheese on the top of each burger

Melt the cheese under the grill

- Put the burgers back under the grill for about a minute, just to melt the cheese slightly

Toast the buns

- Slice the sesame buns in half
- Toast the buns on a baking tray under the grill until lightly browned

Serve

- Add some lettuce to the base of each bun
- Add a spoonful of the sauce, the burger and finish with the top of the bun
- We have used sandwich sticks to hold the burgers together – they are safer than cocktail sticks

Image taken from video

Spicy Crumbed Chicken Nuggets

100% chicken breast with a Chinese five-spice coating, served with fresh spinach and our special BBQ sauce. Spicy Crumbed Chicken Nuggets are a healthier alternative to their ready-made counterparts and are guaranteed to delight your children.

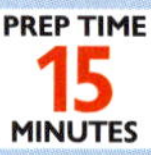

Ingredients

- 2 large chicken breasts
- 100g plain flour
- 2 eggs
- 4 slices bread (to make about 200g fresh breadcrumbs)
- 10g Chinese five spice
- 50g butter (for pan frying)
- 1 tablespoon oil

For the sauce

- 1 tablespoon English mustard
- 2 tablespoon tomato sauce (ketchup)
- 1 tablespoon Worcester sauce
- 2 tablespoon brown sugar

- 50g baby spinach leaves

Utensils

- food processor (for breadcrumbs)
- 2 forks
- medium mixing bowl
- 2 large mixing bowls
- frying pan
- small saucepan
- tablespoon
- small bowls (for serving the sauce)
- wooden spoon
- chopping knife
- chopping board
- small chopping knife

A typical serving contains (based on the max. number of people this recipe serves):

Calories	Sugar	Fat	Saturates	Salt
559	12g	20g	8.0g	1.9g
31%	14%	28%	40%	47%

of a child's guideline daily amount

Step 1 Prepare the nuggets

Make the breadcrumbs

- Remove the crusts from the bread
- Chop the bread into chunks

Put the bread in the blender

- Put the chunks of bread into the blender

Blend

- Blend the breadcrumbs for about 20 seconds

Put in a bowl

- Put the breadcrumbs into a mixing bowl

Add the Chinese five spice

- Add the Chinese five spice to the bowl with the breadcrumbs

Mix

- Mix the breadcrumbs and the five spice together thoroughly

Beat the eggs

- Crack the 2 eggs into a medium mixing bowl and beat them thoroughly

Season

- Season the eggs with salt and pepper

Put the flour in a bowl

- Put the 100g plain flour into another mixing bowl
- Season the flour with salt and pepper

Slice the chicken breasts

- Slice the chicken breasts lengthways

Cut into nuggets

- Cut the chicken into nugget-sized chunks

Step 2 Make the sauce

Put a saucepan on a medium heat

- Add the Worcester sauce
- Add the brown sugar

Add the ketchup

- Add the tomato ketchup to the saucepan

Add the mustard

- Add the English mustard to the pan as well

Mix together

- As the sauce is heating, mix it together

Bring to the boil

- Bring the sauce to the boil, give it another quick mix, then turn off the heat

Pour into small bowls

- Put the sauce into small bowls to cool
- The sauce will be served in these bowls

Coat the nuggets

Coat in flour

- To coat the nuggets, first put them in the bowl of flour
- Use your left hand to do this

Shake off the excess

- Completely coat the chicken in the flour and shake off the excess

Coat in egg

- Next, add the floured chicken to the egg in the second mixing bowl
- Again, use only your left hand. Keep your right hand dry so you can coat the chicken in the breadcrumbs without them sticking to you!

Drop into the breadcrumbs

- Drop the egg-covered nuggets into the breadcrumb bowl
- Make sure you don't get any breadcrumbs on your left hand, or they will stick

Cover in breadcrumbs

- Use your right hand to carefully coat the chicken in the breadcrumb mix
- Make sure they are completely covered

Put on a plate

- Put the nuggets onto a clean plate ready for cooking

Don't stack them!

- Make sure you don't stack the nuggets on top of each other, as they might stick together

Cook & serve

Heat the butter and oil

- Put the 50g of butter and the tablespoon of olive oil in a large frying pan
- Turn the pan to a medium heat

Add the nuggets

- When the butter is foaming, carefully add the chicken nuggets to the pan
- Be very careful when doing this as the pan will be hot!

Turn

- After a couple of minutes, turn the nuggets when they are browned on the underside

Turn again

- Turn the nuggets again after another couple of minutes
- Keep turning the nuggets and moving them around, so they don't burn and to cook them through

Test the nuggets

- Cut one of the larger nuggets open to test if it is cooked
- The nuggets should be white all the way through when they're ready

Drain on kitchen roll

- When cooked, put the nuggets onto some kitchen roll
- This will absorb any excess oil or butter
- Turn off the heat

Plate the spinach and BBQ sauce

- Put a bed of spinach leaves and a small bowl of sauce on a plate

Serve

- Add the nuggets and serve!

image taken from video

Home-Made Bangers and Creamy Mash

with Home-Made Chunky Onion Gravy

The classic British dish utilising home-made pork, sage and onion sausages, creamy mash and healthy onion gravy.

PREP TIME 30 MINUTES | COOK TIME 30 MINUTES | SERVES 4 PEOPLE

RATING   

Ingredients

For the sausages

- 1 slice white bread
- 1 onion
- 10g butter
- ½ an egg
- 400g pork mince (or belly pork)
- pinch of ground mace or nutmeg
- 1 tablespoon of fresh or dried sage
- salt and pepper
- 1 tablespoon olive oil
- flour for dusting

For the chunky onion gravy

- 2 onions
- ½ a chicken stock cube
- 2 tablespoons balsamic vinegar
- 300ml water
- 1 tablespoon olive oil

- parsley to serve

For the creamy mash

- 400g potatoes (maris piper)
- 50g butter
- 50ml single cream
- salt and pepper

Utensils

- food processor
- large mixing bowl
- small chopping knife
- chopping board
- 3 medium/small saucepans
- mixing bowl
- fork
- small frying pan
- peeler
- chopping knife
- measuring jug
- sieve
- spatula
- potato masher
- ladle

A typical serving contains (based on the max. number of people this recipe serves):

Calories	Sugar	Fat	Saturates	Salt
494	7.5g	31g	14g	0.8g
27%	9%	44%	70%	20%

of a child's guideline daily amount

Make the sausages

Remove the crusts from the bread

- To make the breadcrumbs, first remove the crusts from the bread
- Cut the bread into small pieces

Put the bread in the blender

- Put the chunks of bread in the food processor

Blend for 20 seconds

- Use the processor for about 20 seconds to make the breadcrumbs
- Put the breadcrumbs in a bowl and keep them to one side until later

Peel and chop the onion

- To make the sausages, first peel and finely chop the onion

Add the butter to the pan

- Put a medium saucepan on a medium heat and melt the 10g of butter in it

Fry the onions until translucent

- When the butter is foaming, add the onions and fry for a few minutes
- When the onions are translucent, take them off the heat

Beat the egg

- Crack the egg into a small bowl and beat it

Split the egg in half

- Split the egg in half

Put the pork in the processor

- Put the pork mince in the food processor

Add the breadcrumbs

- Add the breadcrumbs

Add the fried onions and ½ egg

- Add the fried onions and the ½ egg to the mixer

Add the spices

- Add a pinch of nutmeg or mace to the mixer, then add the dried sage as well (if you are using fresh sage, chop it then add it to the mixer)

Season

- Season the ingredients with salt and pepper

Blend

- Blend for 40 seconds to mix everything together
- But don't mix for longer than 1½ minutes as the mix will become too soft to form into sausages

Test

- Put a frying pan on a medium heat
- Take a little of the sausage meat and cook it in the frying pan
- Taste the cooked piece of meat and season the mix again if you need to

Put the mix on a floured table

- Sprinkle the work surface with a little flour – this helps stop the meat sticking to the table, or your hands
- Turn the mix out onto the table

Flour the mix and roll it out

- Make sure the mix is covered in flour and roll it into a large sausage shape

Split it in half

- Split the sausage meat in half

Roll out one half of the mix

- Roll one half of the mix into a sausage shape

Split it into 6 pieces

- Split the mix into 6 equal pieces

Roll into small balls

- Roll each piece into a small ball

Roll into sausage shapes

- Roll each ball into a sausage shape on the work surface
- Again, make sure the work surface is floured so they don't stick

Repeat for other half of the mix

- Repeat this process for the other half of the mix

You should have about 12 sausages

- The mix should make about 12 good-sized sausages

Step 2 Prepare the potatoes

Peel the potatoes

- Peel the potatoes with a vegetable peeler

Chop them into chunks

- Cut the potatoes into chunks and put them in a bowl of cold water to remove some of the starch

Put them in a pan

- Then put the potato chunks in a medium saucepan and cover with clean, cold water

Add salt

- Add a pinch of salt

Put the lid on and boil

- Put the lid on the pan and turn the heat to medium and bring the water to the boil
- Once its boiled, turn the heat to low and simmer for 10–15 minutes until the potatoes are cooked

Make the onion gravy

Peel and slice the onions

- First, peel the onions then chop them into thick slices

Put some oil in a pan

- Heat a little olive oil on a medium to high heat in a saucepan

Add the onions and fry

- When the pan is hot, add the onions and fry them until they turn brown

Cook until they brown

- Cooking the onions until they brown like this will help add colour to the gravy

Add the balsamic vinegar

- When the onions have browned, add the 2 tablespoons of balsamic vinegar and give the saucepan a quick stir

Add the water

- Add the 300ml water

Add a stock cube

- Crumble the ½ stock cube into it
- Bring the gravy to the boil and simmer for 8–10 minutes

Step 4 Drain the potatoes

Test the potatoes

- The potatoes should be soft and fall off the knife when cooked
- Turn off the heat for this pan

Drain

- Drain the potatoes

Put them back in the pan

- Put them back in the now dry pan and keep them to one side until later

Cook the sausages

Add some oil to the frying pan

- Put a frying pan on a medium heat and add the tablespoon of olive oil

Add the sausages and cook

- Carefully add the sausages

Keep turning

- Keep turning them so they brown easily

They should be browned all over

- After about 10 minutes, the sausages should be cooked and browned all over
- Turn off the heat and put the lid on the pan to keep them warm

Step 6

Finish the mash & gravy

Put the potatoes back on the heat

- Put the potatoes in the pan back on a medium heat to dry them out so they aren't too soggy when you mash them
- You only need to cook them for a minute or so

Turn off the heat

- Turn off the heat when done

Add the butter

- Then add the butter to the potatoes

Mash

- Mash the potatoes thoroughly

Add the cream

- Add the cream to the potatoes

Mix well

- Mix the cream in with a wooden spoon until the potatoes are smooth

Season and mix again

- Season the mash with salt and pepper and mix well

Check the gravy after 10 minutes

- Make sure you check the gravy after 10 minutes cooking – it should be ready

Put mash and sausages on a plate

- Spoon a dollop of mash into the centre of each plate or bowl
- Put a few sausages on top of the mash

Add the gravy

- Then ladle over the chunky onion gravy

Serve

- Finish with a sprig of parsley for decoration
- Serve and enjoy!

image taken from video

Oven-Baked Pork Meatballs *with Fresh Tomato Sauce*

Fresh pork, onion and garlic meatballs oven-baked in a home-made tomato sauce.

PREP TIME **30** MINUTES

COOK TIME **25** MINUTES

SERVES **4** PEOPLE

RATING   

Ingredients

For the meatballs

- 2 slices bread
- 1 medium onion
- 1 clove of garlic
- ½ a tablespoon olive oil
- 500g pork mince
- 1 egg
- salt and pepper
- a little flour

For the tomato sauce

- 1 onion
- 1 clove of garlic
- ½ tablespoon olive oil
- 20ml white wine vinegar
- 20g caster sugar
- 1 x 400g tin chopped tomatoes
- 100ml water

- crusty bread and parsley to serve

Utensils

- chopping knife
- chopping board
- small chopping knife
- food processor
- small saucepan (with lid)
- wooden spoon
- small mixing bowl
- large mixing bowl
- small frying pan
- spatula
- oven dish
- serving spoon

A typical serving contains (based on the max. number of people this recipe serves):

Calories	Sugar	Fat	Saturates	Salt
338	11g	17g	5g	0.5g
19%	13%	24%	25%	12%

of a child's guideline daily amount

Make the meatball mix

Make the breadcrumbs

- You can buy dried breadcrumbs, not fresh – in this case we need to use fresh breadcrumbs
- Remove the crusts from the bread
- Cut it into small pieces

Put the bread chunks in a blender

- Then put the chunks of bread in the food processor

Blend

- Use the processor for about 20 seconds to make the breadcrumbs

Put them to one side

- Put the breadcrumbs to one side until you need them

Peel and chop the onion finely

- Peel the onion and chop it finely

Crush and peel the garlic

- Crush the garlic under your knife to remove the skin

Chop it finely

- Chop the garlic finely

Turn on the heat and add the oil

- Put a small saucepan on a medium heat and add the ½ tablespoon of olive oil

Add the onion and garlic and fry

- Add the onions and garlic to the pan and fry for 2–3 minutes
- Fry the onion and garlic lightly, so they don't colour

Put them in a small bowl

- When they're cooked, put them in a small bowl and leave them to cool
- Turn off the heat

Put the pork in a large mixing bowl

- Put the pork mince in a large mixing bowl
- Add the onions and garlic to the pork

Crack the egg into the bowl

- Crack the egg into the bowl with the pork, onions and garlic

Season

- Season with salt and pepper

Mix together

- Mix the ingredients together using your hands

Add the breadcrumbs

- Then add the breadcrumbs

Mix thoroughly

- Mix well until completely combined

Test a small piece

- Take a small piece of the meatball mix and cook it in a small frying pan on a medium heat
- After it is cooked, taste it and check the seasoning is right before you make all of the meatballs

Season again if needed

- If you need to, add more seasoning to the meatball mix
- Remember to turn off the heat

Make the meatballs

Flour the table

- Sprinkle a little flour onto the work surface

Cover the ball of mix in flour

- Make a ball of the mix, rolling it in the flour as you go to stop it sticking to your hands

Roll 'balls' from the mix

- Now make the meatballs from the mix
- Again, keep them well floured
- The balls should be a bit smaller than golf balls in size

You should make 12–20

- Make as many balls as you can with the mix (you should be able to make 12–20, depending on how big you make them)

Put them in the oven dish

- Put the meatballs in a large oven dish and put them to one side until you need to cook them

Step 3 Make the tomato sauce

Peel and chop the onion

- Peel and chop the onion finely

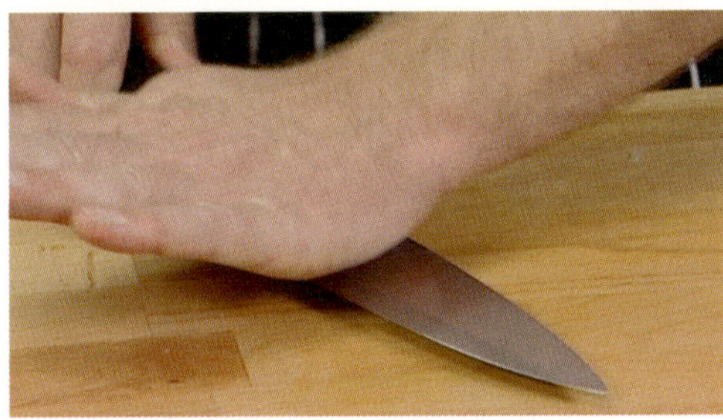

Crush the garlic

- Crush the garlic under your knife – this will make it easier to remove the skin

Peel the garlic

- Peel the skin off the garlic

Chop it finely

- Chop the garlic finely

Add a little oil to the pan

- Put the same saucepan used to cook the onions back on a medium heat and add a little olive oil

Add the onion and garlic and fry

- Add the onions and garlic to the saucepan and fry for a couple of minutes

Add the white wine vinegar and stir

- Add the white wine vinegar and mix it in

Add the caster sugar and stir

- Then add the caster sugar to the saucepan

Add the tomatoes and mix

- Give the saucepan a quick stir and then add the tomatoes

Simmer for 10–15 minutes

- Let the sauce simmer and reduce for about 10 minutes
- Stir occasionally

Cook the meatballs

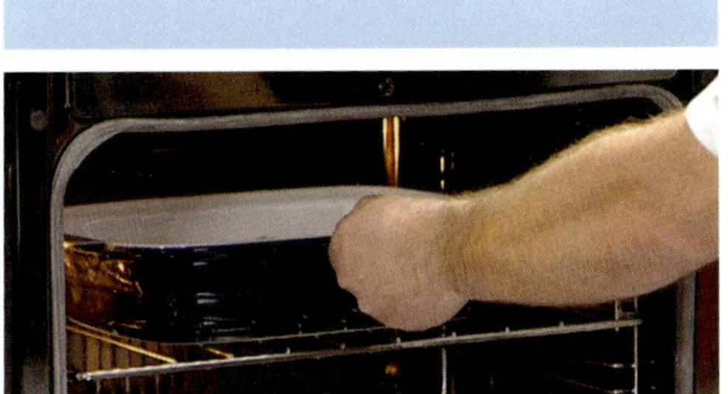

Put the meatballs in the oven

- Now it's time to cook the meatballs
- Put them in the oven at 200°C (400°F or gas mark 6) for 10 minutes

Finish & serve

Add the water to the tomato sauce

- When the tomato sauce has reduced, add the 100ml water

Season and mix

- Season with salt and pepper and mix together
- Turn off the heat

Pour it into the food processor

- Pour the sauce into a food processor

Blend until smooth

- Blend it for about 30 seconds to make it smooth
- Make sure you put a cloth on the top when you do this so no mixture splashes out
- Blending the sauce will help it coat the meatballs better when served

Take the meatballs out of the oven

- When the meatballs are browned all over they are cooked
- Take them out of the oven

Cover the meatballs in the sauce

- Pour the smooth sauce over the meatballs in the oven dish and season with salt and pepper

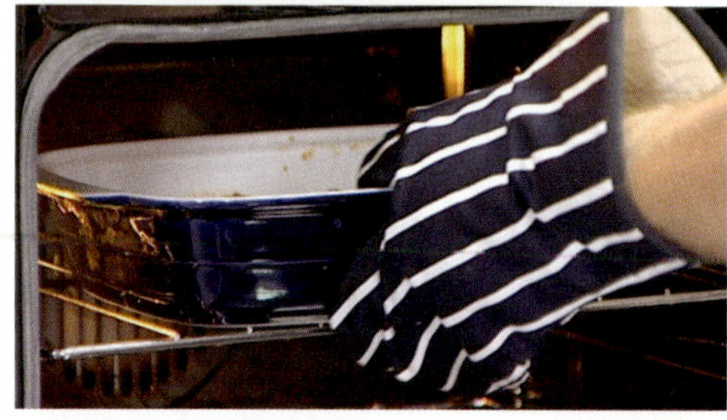

Put the dish back in the oven

- Put it back in the oven for another 10 minutes

Remove and spoon onto a plate

- After 10 minutes, remove the meatballs from the oven
- Spoon the meatballs and sauce into the bowls
- Turn off the oven

Serve

- Serve with crusty bread and a little parsley for decoration
- This is also great with rice or pasta

Image taken from video

Smoked Haddock and Pea Fish Cakes

with Stir-Fried Pak Choi

East meets West with a classic fish cake containing peas, served with stir-fried pak choi.

PREP TIME 30 MINUTES

COOK TIME 30 MINUTES

SERVES 4 PEOPLE

RATING

Ingredients

For the fish cakes

- 400g potatoes
- 50g butter
- 200g fresh smoked haddock (dyed or un-dyed)
- 100g frozen peas
- salt and pepper
- 50g plain flour (for coating)
- olive oil (for frying)
- 2 whole pak choi
- 30ml sesame oil

Utensils

- vegetable peeler
- large mixing bowl
- chopping knife
- chopping board
- medium saucepan
- baking tray or oven dish
- tin foil
- small saucepan
- sieve
- potato masher
- wooden spoon
- 2 forks
- metal ring
- palette knife
- plate
- large frying pan with lid
- silicone spatula/spoon
- tongs

A typical serving contains (based on the max. number of people this recipe serves):

Calories	Sugar	Fat	Saturates	Salt
395	2.0g	25g	9.0g	1.3g
22%	2%	36%	45%	32%

of a child's guideline daily amount

Prepare the potatoes

Peel the potatoes

- Peel the potatoes with a vegetable peeler

Chop them into chunks

- Chop the potatoes into chunks
- Put them in a bowl of cold water to remove some of the starch in them

Put them in a saucepan

- Remove them from the water and put them in a medium saucepan and cover with clean, cold water
- Add a pinch of salt

Put the lid on and bring to the boil

- Turn the heat on to medium and bring the potatoes to the boil with the lid on
- Then turn the heat down to low and simmer for 10–15 minutes until they are cooked

Cook the fish & peas

Rub butter inside the oven dish

- Lightly butter a large baking tray or oven dish
- Put the fish in the dish

Add butter

- Put a few dots of butter on the fish

Cover with tin foil

- Cover the dish with tin foil

Put the fish in the oven

- Bake the fish in a pre-heated oven at 180°C (350°F or gas mark 4) for 8–10 minutes

Add the peas to boiling water

- Bring a small saucepan of water to the boil
- Add a pinch of salt, then add the peas

Boil for 4 minutes

- Boil the peas for about 4 minutes

Drain the peas

- When the peas are cooked, drain them through a sieve
- Turn off the heat

Put to one side

- Put the peas into a mixing bowl and put them to one side

Step 3 Make the fish cakes

Test the potatoes

- They should be soft and should fall off the knife when they are cooked

Drain the potatoes

- Drain the potatoes through a sieve

Put them back in the pan to dry

- Put them back in the pan on a medium heat to dry them out so they aren't too soggy when you mash them

Add the butter and mash

- Turn off the heat
- Add the butter and mash them thoroughly

Mix until smooth

- Mix the potato with a wooden spoon until it's smooth

Mix in the peas and put in a bowl

- Put the cooked peas in the mash and mix them in thoroughly
- Then put the peas and mash in a mixing bowl

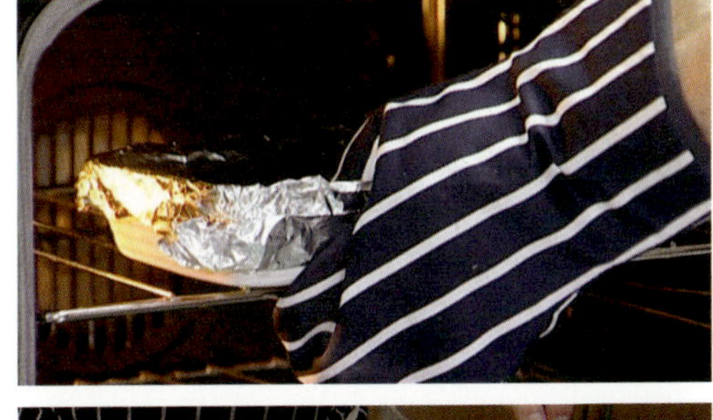

Remove the fish from the oven

- Remove the fish from the oven after 8–10 minutes
- You can tell the fish is cooked as the flesh will be firm and opaque

Flake the fish and put it in the bowl

- Using 2 forks, flake the fish and put it in the mixing bowl

Make sure you check for bones

- When you flake the fish, you can see and remove all of the bones from it before you add it to the mix

Mix everything together thoroughly

- Mix the haddock into the potato and peas thoroughly
- Season with salt and pepper

Turn out the mix

- Sprinkle a little flour into the work surface and turn out the mix

Roll into a sausage shape

- Cover the mix in flour and roll it into a sausage shape

Cut into 4

- Split the mix into 4
- Roll each of the balls around in the flour to coat them

Press into the metal ring

- Press each one into a metal ring to get the shape

Neaten with a palette knife

- Neaten the edges of the fish cakes with a palette knife

Put them in the fridge

- Put the cakes on a floured plate
- Ideally you should put the fish cakes in the fridge for about an hour before you cook them so they will be a bit firmer and less likely to break apart when cooking

Step 4 Cook the fish cakes & pak choi

Prepare the pak choi

- Take the pak choi and chop the end off

Chop them into quarters

- Chop them in half lengthways, then into quarters

Remove the core

- Remove the core and cut any large pieces in half
- Separate the leaves out

Wash the pak choi

- Wash the pak choi quickly in clean water

Cook the fish cakes

- Put a frying pan on a medium heat with a little olive oil
- When the pan is hot, carefully add the fish cakes and fry for about 10 minutes

Turn when browned underneath

- When they have lightly browned on one side, turn them over to cook the other side

Keep turning them

- Keep turning the fish cakes as they cook to make sure you cook them through

Remove them once they've cooked

- After 10 minutes the fish cakes should be cooked, put them on a plate and put them in a low heated oven to keep them warm while we make the stir-fry
- Turn off the heat for the pan

Add the pak choi to a clean pan

- Pour the toasted sesame oil in a clean frying pan on a medium heat
- When hot, add the pak choi

Add salt and stir-fry

- Add a pinch of salt and stir-fry for 2–3 minutes

Put the lid on

- Put the lid on the pan to cook the pak choi through for a few minutes

The pak choi should be tender

- The pak choi should be tender when cooked
- Turn off the heat

Serve

Put the pak choi in a metal ring

- Put a bed of the pak choi on a plate in a metal ring

Top with a fish cake

- Carefully remove the metal ring and sit the fish cake on top

Serve

- Top with more pak choi and sesame oil
- That's it!

image taken from video

Lasagne Pots

Individual portions of lean minced beef, pasta and creamy cheese sauce served with crusty bread.

Ingredients

- 1 large or 2 small onions
- 1 large or 2 small cloves of garlic
- 1 tablespoon olive oil
- 500g lean minced beef
- 4 tablespoons (60ml/ ¼ cup) beef stock
- 2 x 400g tins chopped tomatoes
- 1 tablespoon fresh or dried oregano
- salt and black pepper
- 4 sheets easy-cook lasagne
- 25g Parmesan cheese
- crusty bread to serve
- a few sprigs of parsley to serve

For the cheese sauce

- 40g butter
- 40g plain flour
- 500ml semi-skimmed milk
- 50g gruyere cheese (grated)
- salt and ground white pepper

Utensils

- small chopping knife
- chopping board
- chopping knife
- 2 medium saucepans
- wooden spoon
- spatula
- 1 small saucepan
- lasagne pots (small individual pots)
- metal cutters/rings
- ladle
- large baking tray

A typical serving contains (based on the max. number of people this recipe serves):

Calories	Sugar	Fat	Saturates	Salt
345	7.0g	22g	10g	0.5g
19%	8%	31%	50%	12%

of a child's guideline daily amount

Make the sauce/cook the pasta

Peel and halve the onion

- First peel the onion and chop it in half

Slice it horizontally

- Lay one half flat and slice it 2 or 3 times horizontally

Chop along the core

- Then slice the onion along the core, but not all the way to the end as we want it to stay held together

Turn through 90° to dice finely

- Then turn the onion through 90° and dice it finely

Peel the garlic

- Crush the garlic under your knife to remove the skin

Chop it finely

- Chop the garlic finely

Add the oil to the pan

- Put a saucepan on a medium heat and add a little olive oil

Add the onion and garlic

- Add the chopped onion and garlic to the olive oil in the pan

Fry until translucent

- Fry them for a few minutes until they are translucent

Add the mince and break it up

- When the onion and garlic have slightly browned, add the minced beef to the pan and break it up so it doesn't stick together

Fry until it's browned or 'sealed'

- Fry the beef until it's browned all over, stirring occasionally

Add the beef stock

- When it is all browned, add the beef stock

Add the tomatoes and oregano

- Then add the 2 tins of chopped tomatoes and the oregano

Mix and season

- Mix the sauce together well and season with salt and pepper

Put the lid on and simmer

- Bring the sauce to the boil and cover
- Simmer for about 15 minutes, stirring occasionally

Add oil to boiling, salted water

- Bring a pan of water to the boil and add a little olive oil and a pinch of salt

Add the pasta sheets, one at a time

- Add the pasta sheets, one at a time, to the boiling water and cook them for about 15 minutes (or as directed on the packet)

Keep the pasta sheets turning

- Turn the pasta sheets in the water to help prevent them sticking together

Put the pasta sheets in cold water

- When they are cooked, remove the pasta sheets from the boiling water and put them in a large bowl of cold water to stop them cooking and help keep them separate
- Turn off the heat

Step 2 Make the cheese sauce

Add 40g butter to a small saucepan

- While the tomato sauce is simmering, you can make the cheese sauce
- Put a small saucepan on a medium heat and add the 40g of butter

When foaming, add the flour

- When the butter has melted and is foaming, add the flour and mix vigorously with a wooden spoon until it forms a paste

Then add the milk, a little at a time

- Then add the cold milk, a little at a time, mixing as you go

Mix until combined

- Each time, mix the milk in until it is completely combined

Add more milk

- When the milk has mixed with the sauce, add a bit more milk and mix well again

Keep adding milk and stirring

- You want to beat out the lumps in the sauce, so keep stirring!
- Keep going until all the milk is used and the sauce is smooth and creamy

Then bring to the boil

- Bring the sauce to the boil, stirring continuously

Add the cheese and stir

- Add the grated cheese to the sauce and continue to stir constantly to melt the cheese

Season with salt and white pepper

- Season the sauce with salt and ground white pepper and mix in
- Then let it simmer gently for about 5 minutes, stirring occasionally so it doesn't stick to the bottom of the pan

It should look like this

- The sauce should be thick, creamy and smooth

Build & cook the pots

Put the lasagne sauce in the pots

- Put some of the lasagne sauce at the bottom of your pots

Cut circles from the pasta sheets

- Cut circles out of the pasta sheets with a metal ring

Put a circle in each pot

- Put one of the pasta circles in each pot

Top with more lasagne sauce

- Add another layer of the lasagne sauce

Add another pasta circle

- Add another pasta circle on top of that

Then add the cheese sauce

- Ladle the cheese sauce on the top

Finish with a sprinkle of Parmesan

- Cover the tops of each one with a sprinkling of Parmesan cheese

Put the lasagne pots in the oven

- Put the lasagne pots on a large baking tray then cook in a pre-heated oven for about ½ an hour at 180°C (350°F or gas mark 4)

Cooked

- When cooked they will be lightly browned on the top
- Turn off the oven

Serve with crusty bread

- When they are done, serve them in the pots on a plate with crusty bread and a sprig of parsley for decoration

image taken from video

Super Thin Pizzas

with 3 Toppings

A favourite thin and crispy pizza base topped with mushroom and thyme, Cajun chicken and sweetcorn, or ham, onion and tomato.

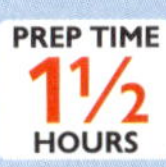
PREP TIME 1½ HOURS

COOK TIME 30 MINUTES

SERVES 4–6 PEOPLE

RATING

Ingredients

For the basic pizza dough
- 200ml warm water
- ½ teaspoon of salt
- 7g dried yeast
- 1 teaspoon caster sugar
- 375g bread flour (or plain flour)
- 2 tablespoons olive oil

For the tomato sauce
- 1 onion
- 1 clove of garlic
- 4 ripe tomatoes
- 1 tablespoon olive oil
- 20ml white wine vinegar
- 20g caster sugar
- 50g tomato purée (or 1 jar tomato pasta sauce)

Mushroom and thyme topping
- 150g button mushrooms
- 1 teaspoon thyme leaves
- 1 tablespoon olive oil
- 150g half fat mozzarella cheese

Ham, onion and tomato topping
- ½ a medium or 1 small onion
- 2 tomatoes
- 2 slices ham (about 100g)
- 150g half fat mozzarella cheese
- pinch of oregano

Cajun chicken and sweetcorn topping
- 150g cooked chicken
- 100g sweetcorn
- 1 teaspoon Cajun spice
- pinch of salt
- 150g half fat mozzarella cheese

Utensils

- measuring jug
- whisk
- cling film
- small chopping knife
- chopping board
- chopping knife
- medium saucepan with lid
- wooden spoon
- 2 large mixing bowls
- food processor or blender
- rolling pin
- flat baking tray or pizza trays
- pizza cutter

A typical serving contains (based on the max. number of people this recipe serves):

Calories	Sugar	Fat	Saturates	Salt
522	6.0g	20g	9.0g	1.2g
29%	7%	28%	45%	31%

of a child's guideline daily amount

Start the pizza dough

Prepare the yeast

- Put the warm water in a jug and add the salt, dried yeast and sugar
- The water should be about body temperature

Whisk thoroughly

- Whisk thoroughly to dissolve the yeast
- Cover the jug with cling film and put in a warm place to prove – it will froth up and a foam will form on top of the yeast mixture

Put the jug in a warm place

- It will take 10–20 minutes to prove, depending on how warm the place is
- We have put it into the top of a double oven that is not on but is warm as the bottom oven is on – you could also put it in the airing cupboard!

Start the tomato sauce

Peel and halve the onion

- While the pizza dough is proving, you can make the tomato sauce
- Peel the onion and halve it

Slice it horizontally

- Slice the onion horizontally with your hand flat on the top

Dice the onion

- Slice the onion along the core but not all the way to the end
- Then turn the onion through 90° and dice it finely

Peel the garlic

- Crush a clove of garlic under your knife to remove the skin

Chop it finely

- Chop the garlic finely

Halve, then quarter the tomatoes

- Remove the tomatoes from the vine
- Halve the tomatoes, then quarter them

Cut into chunks

- Cut the tomatoes into small chunks

Put the onion and garlic in a pan

- Put the olive oil in a medium saucepan on a medium heat
- Add the garlic and onion to the saucepan

Fry until translucent

- Fry them in the oil for couple of minutes until they are translucent

Add vinegar and caster sugar

- Add the white wine vinegar and the caster sugar to the saucepan

Add the tomatoes

- Then add the chopped tomatoes and stir them in

Add the tomato purée

- Add the tomato purée

Mix well

- Mix all the ingredients together

Put the lid on and simmer

- Put the lid on the pan and let the tomatoes cook down and simmer for about 10 minutes, stirring occasionally until the sauce thickens up

Make the dough

Remove the jug

- After 10 minutes, remove the jug from the warm place and take off the cling film

It should have a foam on top

- There should be a foam on top of the yeast mixture

Add the yeast mix to the flour

- Put the flour in the large mixing bowl, make a well in the middle of the flour and carefully pour in the yeast mixture

Add the olive oil

- Add the olive oil as well

Mix together

- Mix it with your hands until it comes together

Turn the dough out onto the table

- Take the dough the out of the bowl and put it on the work surface

Knead the dough

- Knead the dough continuously for about 3–5 minutes until it is smooth and firm

Keep going!

- It is worth the effort!

It should become smooth

- The dough should be firm and have a smooth surface
- Make it into a ball shape

Flour a clean bowl

- Sprinkle flour into a large, clean mixing bowl

Put the dough in the bowl

- Put it in the lightly-floured bowl and press it down gently
- Cover the bowl with cling film

Leave the dough to 'prove'

- Put it in the warm place you used before for the yeast mixture
- Leave it to prove – it should rise and double in size in about an hour

Finish the sauce

Check the sauce after 10 minutes

- After 10 minutes, the sauce will have cooked down
- Turn off the heat

Put it in a blender and season

- Pour the sauce into a food processor and season it with salt and pepper

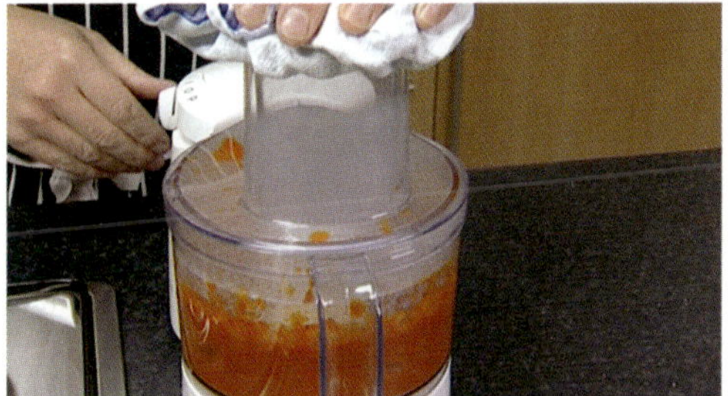

Blend the sauce

- Make sure you hold a tea towel on top to stop the sauce splashing out
- Blend for about a minute until it's smooth

Put it to one side

- Put the sauce in a bowl and put it to one side
- The sauce can be made in advance and be kept in the fridge for 4–5 days

Step 5

Make the pizza bases

Remove the dough

- After an hour, remove the dough from the warm place and take off the cling film

Press some of the air out of it

- Sprinkle the top of the dough with flour and press it down to get some of the air out

Knead it slightly

- Turn it out onto a floured work surface
- Knead the dough for 30 seconds or so to knock the air out of it

Roll it into a sausage shape

- Roll the dough into a rough sausage shape

Cut it into three equal pieces

- Split the dough into 3 equal pieces

Roll each piece out

- Make sure there is flour on the work surface and begin to roll each piece out

Roll into a large circle

- Roll each piece into a large circle, as thin as you can
- Make sure you use plenty of flour so the dough doesn't stick

It should be very thin

- You want to get the dough as thin as possible

Put it on a pizza tray

- Put each pizza base on a flat baking tray or pizza tray

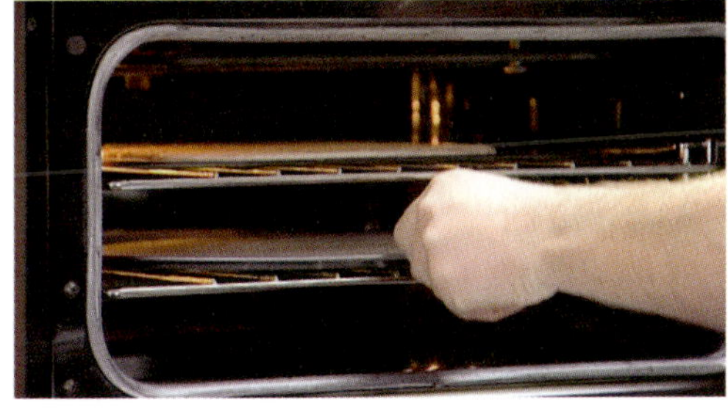

Put the bases in the warm place

- Put the bases back in the warm place to let them rise slightly again for another 10–15 minutes
- If you don't have enough baking trays, make one at a time – put the other 2 in the fridge to stop them rising more

The bases will have risen slightly

- The pizza bases will have risen slightly in the warm place
- Now you are ready to add the toppings

Prepare the mozzarella

Slice it finely

- You will need mozzarella cheese for all of the toppings
- Cut the mozzarella in half to make it easier to handle
- Lay the cheese on the flat and slice it finely

Mushroom & thyme

Slice the mushrooms

- First, slice the mushrooms thinly

Pick the thyme leaves

- Pick the thyme leaves from the stem

Cook

- Put a small frying pan on a medium heat and add the olive oil
- Add the mushrooms to the frying pan and sauté them

Add the thyme

- Add the thyme leaves to the mushrooms

Fry until lightly browned

- Cook until the mushrooms are lightly browned

Put to one side

- When brown, turn off the heat and put the mushrooms in a bowl to one side

Add the topping to the base

- Spread the tomato sauce over the top of the first pizza base
- Put the mushrooms and thyme on top and spread them evenly across the pizza

Top with slices of mozzarella

- Arrange the sliced mozzarella on the top

Sprinkle with fresh thyme

- Sprinkle a few more fresh thyme leaves over the top of the pizza before cooking
- Go to Step 7 to see how to cook the pizza

Ham, onion and tomato

Peel the onion

- Peel and halve the onion

Slice it finely

- Cut it into thin slices

Slice the tomatoes finely

- Thinly slice the tomatoes

Cut the ham slices in half

- Cut the slices of ham in half

Slice it finely

- Cut the ham into thin strips

Spread tomato sauce over the base

- Spread the tomato sauce all over the second pizza base
- Lay the sliced tomatoes evenly across the top

Add the sliced onions

- Sprinkle the sliced onions on the top

Then the ham

- Then add the chopped ham

Top with mozzarella

- Arrange the sliced mozzarella on the top

Sprinkle with oregano to finish

- Sprinkle the pinch of oregano over the top to finish
- Go to Step 7 to see how to cook the pizza

Cajun chicken & sweetcorn

Slice the chicken

- Cut the chicken into small pieces

Put it in a large mixing bowl

- Put the chicken in a large mixing bowl

Add the sweetcorn and spice

- Add the drained sweetcorn
- Add the Cajun spice

Mix together well

- Mix the ingredients together thoroughly with a spoon

Season

- Season with salt

Spread tomato sauce over the base

- Spread the tomato sauce all over the pizza base
- Put the Cajun chicken mix on the top of the pizza and spread it out evenly

Top with mozzarella

- Arrange the sliced mozzarella on the top

Sprinkle with a little Cajun spice

- Finally, sprinkle a little more of the Cajun spice over the top of the mozzarella
- Go to Step 7 to see how to cook the pizza

Cook the pizzas

Cook the pizzas

- Cook the pizzas in a pre-heated oven at 200°C (400°F or gas mark 6) for about 10–15 minutes
- It is better to cook them on the top shelf as it is hotter, but not essential!

Should be crispy and golden brown

- After 10–15 minutes, take the pizzas out of the oven
- The pizzas should be crispy and golden brown on the top

Image taken from video

Honey and Lemon Chicken Kebabs *with Garlic Bread*

A healthy and tasty way of using chicken thighs with a honey, lemon and plum marinade, served with classic garlic bread.

RATING 

Ingredients

For the kebabs

- 1 lemon (juice and zest)
- 1 tablespoon soy sauce
- 50ml honey
- 30ml vegetable oil
- 1 tablespoon plum sauce
- 4 skinned and boned chicken thighs (you can also use ready diced chicken thigh or breast)

For the garlic bread

- 2g parsley
- 2 cloves of garlic
- salt and pepper
- 80g soft butter
- ½ French stick
- some watercress leaves to serve

Utensils

- cheese grater
- 2 large mixing bowls
- fork
- seive
- whisk
- small chopping knife
- chopping board
- serving spoon
- chopping knife
- bread knife
- palette knife (for spreading)
- tin foil
- large roasting tray
- grill pan
- wooden skewers (soaked in water)

A typical serving contains (based on the max. number of people this recipe serves):

Calories	Sugar	Fat	Saturates	Salt
425	13g	24g	12g	1.7g
24%	15%	34%	60%	42%

of a child's guideline daily amount

Marinate the chicken

Grate the zest from the lemon

- Grate the zest from the lemon and put it in the bowl

Squeeze the juice into the bowl

- Halve the lemon, stick the fork into the flesh of the lemon and squeeze the juice into the bowl through a sieve – be careful not to get any pips in the bowl

Add the soy sauce

- Add the soy sauce to the lemon juice and zest

Add the honey

- Add the honey
- You can warm the honey slightly in the oven or on the hob to make it easier to pour

Add vegetable oil and plum sauce

- Add the vegetable oil and plum sauce

Whisk thoroughly

- Whisk together thoroughly

Prepare the chicken

- Pull the skin off the chicken thighs

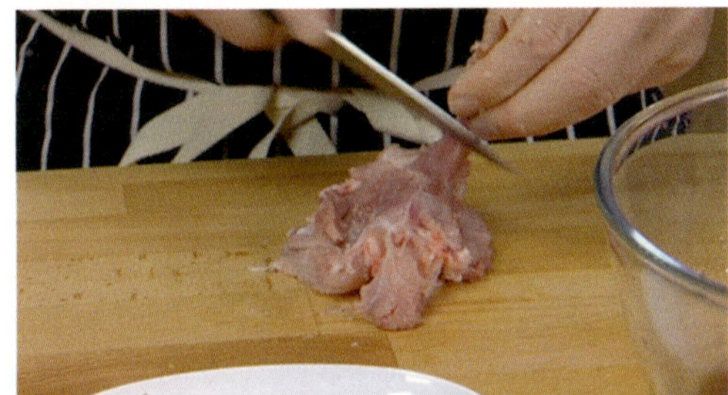

Cut the flesh away from the bone

- Carefully remove the bone from the centre of the thigh using a sharp chopping knife
- Also, make sure you remove any cartilage

Cut into pieces

- Cut the chicken thighs into 4 or 5 pieces and put them into the marinade in the mixing bowl

Season and mix together

- Season with salt and pepper
- Using a serving spoon, mix the chicken into the marinade, making sure it's completely covered

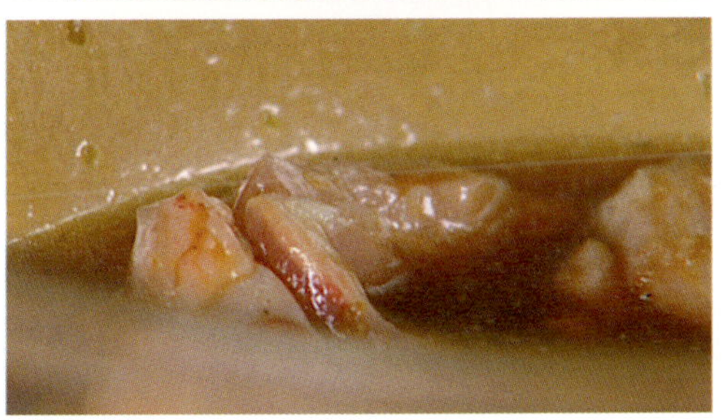

Leave for 10–15 minutes

- Leave the chicken in the marinade for a minimum of 10–15 minutes
- You can prepare the chicken a few hours in advance if you like

Make the garlic bread

Pick the parsley

- Pick the parsley leaves from the stem

Chop finely

- Chop the parsley as finely as possible and put it in a mixing bowl

Peel the garlic

- Crush the garlic under your knife to remove the skin

Chop finely

- Chop the garlic finely

Add salt

- Sprinkle it with a little salt

Crush to a paste

- Using the side of your knife, crush the garlic to a paste
- The salt acts an abrasive surface to break down the garlic
- Put the garlic in the bowl

Add butter

- Add the butter to the bowl with the parsley and garlic

Beat together

- Beat all these ingredients together with a wooden spoon

Add pepper and beat again

- Season with pepper and beat again until combined
- It should be creamy and spreadable
- The butter will last in the fridge for 7–10 days

Slice the bread

- Next, take the French stick and slice it into 2cm pieces
- DON'T slice all the way through the loaf – leave it attached at the bottom

Spread the garlic butter

- Spread the garlic butter in between each slice of the bread and on each end

Wrap the bread in tin foil

- Wrap the garlic bread in tin foil and put it in a roasting tray

Into oven

- Put it in the oven for 10 minutes at 180°C (350°F or gas mark 4)

Step 3 Make & cook the kebabs

Make the kebabs

- Make sure the wooden skewers have been soaked overnight so they won't burn
- After the chicken has marinated, thread it onto the skewers
- Fold any large pieces and put the skewer through twice

Put the kebabs under the grill

- Put the kebabs on a grill tray and grill on high for about 10–15 minutes

Turn halfway through

- Turn the kebabs halfway through cooking
- Keep checking and turning them as they are cooking

Put them back under the grill

- Put them back under the grill to finish cooking

They should be browned all over

- The kebabs should be lightly browned all over when finished

Step 4 Serve

Garnish with some watercress

- Serve the kebabs with some watercress

Garlic bread

- The garlic bread should be golden brown when cooked

Serve

- The kebabs are great served with the garlic bread and a little plum sauce

image taken from video

Veggie Kids' Kebabs
with Coconut Rice

Grilled vegetarian kebabs with a garlic marinade, served with coconut basmati rice and plum sauce.

PREP TIME	COOK TIME	SERVES
20 MINUTES	20 MINUTES	4 PEOPLE

RATING  

Ingredients

- 1 clove of garlic
- pinch of salt
- 50ml olive oil
- salt and pepper
- 1 courgette
- 2 medium red onions
- 1 red pepper
- 1 yellow pepper
- 8 button mushrooms
- 400g basmati rice (you can also use white long grain rice)
- 35g desiccated coconut
- 800ml water (plus warm water to wash the rice)
- plum sauce to serve

Utensils

- chopping knife
- chopping board
- 2 large mixing bowls
- small chopping knife
- wooden skewers (soaked in water)
- grill pan
- sieve
- wooden spoon
- cling film
- microwave
- fork
- serving spoon

A typical serving contains (based on the max. number of people this recipe serves):

Calories	Sugar	Fat	Saturates	Salt
543	8.0g	16g	6.0g	0.02g
30%	9%	23%	30%	0.5%

of a child's guideline daily amount

Make the kebabs

Peel the garlic

- Crush the garlic under your knife to remove the skin

Chop it finely

- Chop the garlic finely

Sprinkle with salt

- Sprinkle it with a little salt

Crush to a paste

- Using the side of your knife, crush the garlic to a paste
- The salt acts as an abrasive surface to break down the garlic

Put it in a bowl with the olive oil

- Put the garlic in a large mixing bowl and add the olive oil

Season

- Season with salt and pepper

Mix together with a fork

Chop the courgette

- Cut the courgette into thick slices, removing the ends, and put the slices in the marinade

Peel and halve the red onions

- Peel the red onions and cut them in half

Chop each half into 4 chunks

- Cut each half into large chunks – about 4 pieces – then put them in the bowl

Prepare the red pepper

- Halve the red pepper and pull out the core

Chop into chunks

- Chop the pepper into chunks and put it in the bowl

Prepare the yellow pepper

- Halve the yellow pepper and pull out the core

Chop into chunks

- Chop the pepper into chunks and put it in the bowl

Add mushrooms and coat

- Wipe the mushrooms and halve them if they are too big
- Add them to the bowl
- Using a large spoon, coat all the vegetables in the marinade – this will help to cook them as well as add to the flavour

Make the kebabs

- Carefully thread the vegetables alternately onto the wooden skewers

Make sure each one is the same

- Make sure all the skewers are the same
- You can make extra if you have any remaining vegetables

Put the kebabs on a grill tray

- Put the kebabs on a grill tray, ready to cook, but don't cook them yet!
- Put them to one side

Make the rice

Wash the rice

- Put the rice in a large mixing bowl and cover it in warm water to wash the starch out of the rice
- Drain the starchy water away and wash the rice again if needed – you might find it easier to wash the rice under the tap

Drain

- Once washed, drain the rice through a sieve

Put it in a clean bowl

- Put the rice in a large, clean mixing bowl
- Add the desiccated coconut

Add the water

- Add the 800ml of water to cook the rice in

Add a pinch of salt

- Add a good pinch of salt and then mix lightly

Wrap the bowl in cling film

- Wrap the bowl in cling film but don't pierce a hole in it

Put the rice in the microwave

- Put the rice in the microwave (800W) on high for 20 minutes

Finish & serve

Put the kebabs under the grill

- Put the kebabs under a hot grill for about 10 minutes

Turn them halfway through

- Turn the kebabs over halfway through cooking

Put them back under the grill

- Put them back under the grill to finish

They should be nicely browned

- When the veggie kebabs are cooked, they will be lightly browned and will have softened slightly
- Turn off the grill

After 20 minutes, remove the rice

- After 20 minutes, you should have fluffy rice
- BE CAREFUL – the bowl will be VERY HOT!

Pierce the cling film

- Cut a hole in the cling film to let the steam out before you uncover it, otherwise you could burn yourself

Fluff the rice with a fork

- Carefully remove the cling film from the bowl
- Fluff the rice with a fork

Serve

- Spoon the rice into the bowls
- Serve the kebabs with the rice and drizzle over some plum sauce to finish

Chicken Piri Piri Kebabs

with a Crunchy Thai Salad

A zingy marinade of lemon, sweet chilli and plum make these kebabs extra interesting – served with a Thai-style salad.

PREP TIME **20** MINUTES

COOK TIME **15** MINUTES

SERVES **4** PEOPLE

RATING     

Ingredients

For the kebabs

- 1 lemon (juice and zest)
- 1 tablespoon soy sauce
- 30ml vegetable oil
- 50ml sweet chilli sauce
- 1 tablespoon plum sauce
- salt and pepper
- 4 chicken thigh fillets

For the salad

- 6 radishes
- ¼ of a gallia melon or large slice of watermelon
- 2 handfuls rocket leaves
- 2 handfuls fresh mint
- 2 handfuls fresh coriander
- 50g peanuts

Utensils

- cheese grater
- 2 medium mixing bowls
- chopping knife
- chopping board
- sieve
- fork
- whisk
- small chopping knife
- kitchen scissors
- serving spoon
- wooden skewers (soaked in water overnight)
- grill tray

A typical serving contains (based on the max. number of people this recipe serves):

Calories	Sugar	Fat	Saturates	Salt
300	13g	15g	3.0g	1.2g
17%	15%	21%	15%	30%

of a child's guideline daily amount

Marinate the chicken

Grate the zest

- Grate the zest from the lemon

Halve the lemon

- Halve the lemon

Squeeze the juice into the bowl

- Stick a fork into the flesh of the lemon and squeeze the juice into a mixing bowl
- Pass the juice though a sieve to catch any pips

Add the soy sauce

- Add the soy sauce to the lemon juice

Add the vegetable oil

- Add the 30ml vegetable oil

Add the sweet chilli sauce

- Add the sweet chilli sauce

Add the plum sauce

- Add the plum sauce to the bowl as well

Season

- Season with salt and pepper

Whisk

- Whisk the marinade together thoroughly

Prepare the chicken

- Pull the skin off the chicken thighs
- Cut off any sinew or fat

Cut the bone away from the meat

- Carefully remove the bones from the centre using a sharp knife
- You can buy boneless or ready-diced chicken thighs – alternatively you can use turkey or pork instead of chicken (but pork takes longer to marinate)

Cut the thigh into 4 pieces

- Cut the thigh meat into large pieces (about 4 pieces per thigh) and put them into the marinade

Coat the chicken in the marinade

- Mix the chicken into the marinade, making sure you completely cover it

Leave for 10–15 minutes

- Leave the chicken in the marinade for a minimum of 10–15 minutes
- You can prepare the chicken a few hours in advance if you like

Step 2

Make the salad

Remove the tops from the radishes

- Cut the stalks off the radishes and give them a quick wash if needed

Halve then slice

- Cut them in half, then finely slice them

Quarter the melon

- Take the gallia melon, cut it into quarters then scoop out the seeds with a spoon
- You can use a watermelon instead of gallia, but it might not be available at all times of the year

Cut into 4 pieces

- Cut the ¼ melon into about 4 pieces

Remove the skin

- Carefully remove the skin by laying the pieces flat on the board and cutting the flesh away

Chop into chunks

- Chop the melon into chunks

Rocket & mint in a bowl

- Take the rocket leaves and put them in a medium mixing bowl
- Using a pair of kitchen scissors, snip the mint leaves from the stems into the bowl
- This will stop the mint getting bruised and will maximise the flavour

Snip the coriander

- Then, snip the coriander leaves from the stems into the bowl

Add the melon and peanuts

- Put the melon chunks and peanuts in the bowl

Add the radishes and mix together

- Add the radishes to the salad as well and mix everything together with the serving spoon

Make sure it's completely mixed

- The salad should be thoroughly mixed

Step 3 Make & cook the kebabs

Make the kebabs

- After 15–20 minutes, carefully thread the chicken onto the soaked skewers
- The skewers are soaked so they don't burn when they go under the grill

Onto grill tray

- Put the kebabs on the grill tray
- You should have enough to make 4 large or 8 small kebabs

Put them under the grill

- Put them under a medium grill for about 10–15 minutes

Turn halfway through cooking

- About halfway through cooking, turn the kebabs over
- Keep checking and turning occasionally

Put them back under the grill to finish

- Put the kebabs back under the grill to finish cooking them

They should be light brown

- Make sure the chicken is cooked all the way through
- They should have turned a light brown colour

Serve

- If you want, just before you serve the salad, season it with salt and pepper and pour on a little olive oil
- Mix the salad together again
- Serve with the kebabs!

Enjoy!

image taken from video

Veggie Lasagne

The ultimate 5-a-day dish. Use any combination of fresh vegetables to create this vegetarian version of the classic Italian dish.

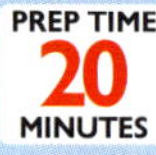

SERVES 4–6 PEOPLE

RATING   

Ingredients

- 1 large or 2 small onions
- 1 large or 2 small cloves of garlic
- 4 button mushrooms
- ½ a medium courgette
- ½ a medium aubergine
- 1 red pepper
- 1 tablespoon olive oil
- 2 x 400g tins chopped tomatoes
- 4 tablespoons vegetable stock
- 1 tablespoon fresh or dried oregano
- salt and black pepper

For the cheese sauce

- 40g butter
- 40g plain flour
- 500ml semi-skimmed milk
- 50g gruyere cheese (grated)
- salt and white pepper
- 6–8 sheets easy-cook lasagne
- 25g Parmesan cheese

Utensils

- small chopping knife
- chopping board
- chopping knife
- 2 medium saucepans
- wooden spoon
- spatula
- small saucepan
- oven-proof dish
- serving spoon
- ladle

A typical serving contains (based on the max. number of people this recipe serves):

Calories	Sugar	Fat	Saturates	Salt
400	17g	34g	11g	0.8g
22%	20%	48%	55%	20%

of a child's guideline daily amount

Step 1 Prepare the vegetables

Peel the onions

- Peel the onions

Slice them horizontally

- Slice the onions horizontally with your hand flat on the top

Slice along the core

- Slice the onions along the core, but not all the way to the end

Turn through 90° and dice

- Turn the onion through 90° and dice finely

Peel the garlic

- Crush the garlic under your knife to remove the skin

Chop it finely

- Chop the garlic finely

Roughly slice the mushrooms

- Roughly slice the button mushrooms

Then dice them finely

- Then dice the mushrooms finely

Cut one side off the courgette

- Cut a strip off one side of the courgette so you can lay it flat – this will make it easier to dice

Lay it flat and slice

- Lay the courgette flat and slice it finely

Cut the slices into strips

- Cut the fine slices into strips

Finely dice the courgette

- Cut the courgette strips into fine dice

Remove the end of the aubergine

- Remove the end of the aubergine

Cut one side off

- Cut one side off the aubergine so you can lay it flat

Lay it flat and slice

- Lay it flat and cut the aubergine into slices

Cut the slices into strips

- Cut the slice of aubergine into fine strips

Finely dice

- Cut the strips into fine dice

Prepare the red pepper

- Halve the red pepper and pull out the core

Cut into quarters, then strips

- Cut it into quarters, then into strips

Dice

- Finely dice the strips

Step 2

Make the lasagne sauce

Add the oil, onions and garlic

- Add the oil, onions and garlic to a pan on a medium heat

Fry

- Fry the onions and garlic for a couple of minutes

Add the red pepper

- Add the red pepper and stir for 1–2 minutes

Add the courgette

- Then add the courgette and stir again

Add the mushrooms

- Add the mushrooms

Add the aubergine

- Add the aubergine and mix together

Cook for 2 minutes

- Cook for 2 minutes, stirring occasionally

Add the chopped tomatoes

- Next, add the chopped tomatoes

Add the vegetable stock

- Then add the vegetable stock

Add the oregano and mix

- Add the oregano and mix the sauce together

Bring to the boil

- Bring to the boil, then stir

Lid on and simmer

- Put the lid on and simmer on a low heat for 10 minutes

Pre-cook the pasta sheets

Add oil to boiling, salted water

- Bring the water in another pan to the boil and add a little olive oil and a pinch of salt

Add the pasta sheets, one at a time

- Add the pasta sheets, one at a time, to the water and cook for about 15 minutes (or as directed on the packet)

Keep them moving

- Keep moving them so they don't stick together

Check the lasagne

- Check the lasagne sauce and give it a quick stir

Put the pasta sheets in cold water

- After 15 minutes, remove the pasta from the pan and put it in a bowl of cold water until we need it
- This will stop the pasta from cooking any more and will also stop it sticking together
- Turn off the heat

Make the cheese sauce

Melt the butter in a saucepan

- Put a small saucepan on a medium heat and add the 40g of butter

Add the flour and mix

- When the butter has melted and is foaming, add the flour and mix vigorously with a wooden spoon until it forms a paste

Add a little milk

- Then add the cold milk, a little at a time, mixing as you go

Mix until combined

- Make sure the milk is completely combined before adding any more
- You want to beat out the lumps in the sauce, so mix vigorously

Use all of the milk

- Each time, when the milk has mixed with the sauce, add a bit more milk and mix well again
- Keep going until all the milk is used

Should be smooth and creamy

- When all the milk is used, the sauce should go smooth and creamy

Bring to the boil

- Bring the sauce to the boil, stirring continuously

Add the cheese

- Then add the grated cheese to the sauce
- Continue to stir constantly to melt the cheese

Season

- Season with salt and ground white pepper

It should be thick and smooth

- Let it simmer gently for about 5 minutes, stirring occasionally so it doesn't stick to the bottom of the pan
- The sauce should be thick and smooth when finished
- Turn off the heat

Build & cook the lasagne

Season the sauce if needed

- Taste the lasagne sauce before you add it to the oven dish to see if it needs any more seasoning

Add the sauce to the oven dish

- Spoon a layer of the lasagne sauce into the bottom of the oven dish
- Using a serving spoon to spread it out so that it covers the base of the dish

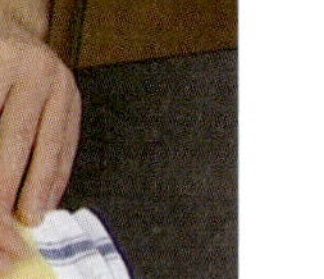

Drain the pasta sheets

- Dry the pasta on a clean cloth before you put it in the dish – this will stop it going soggy when we bake it

Add the pasta sheets

- Cover the first layer of the lasagne sauce with the pasta sheets

Add another layer of sauce

- Then put another layer of the lasagne sauce over the pasta sheets

Top with remaining pasta sheets

- Cover the sauce again with the remaining pasta sheets

Add the cheese sauce

- Ladle the cheese sauce over the top of the lasagne
- Spread it out to the edges of the dish with a spoon, making sure you tuck in any bits of pasta that are sticking up

Sprinkle Parmesan over the top

- Sprinkle the top with Parmesan cheese

Put it in the oven

- Bake in the top of the oven at 180°C (350°F or gas mark 4) for about 20 minutes
- You can make the lasagne in advance and keep it in the fridge

Step 6 Serve

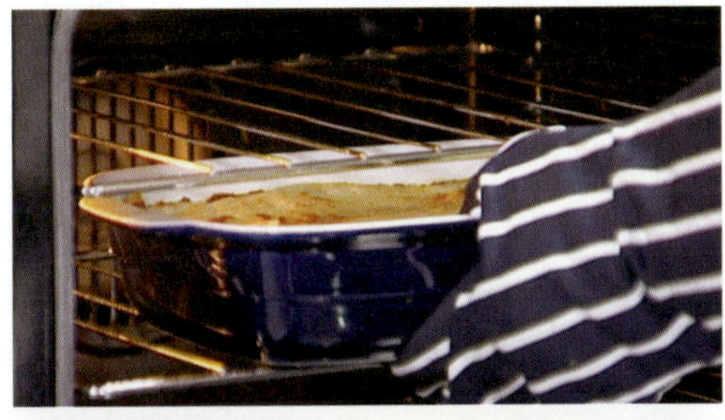

Remove the lasagne from the oven

- After 20 minutes, remove the lasagne from the oven

It should be golden brown on top

- When it's ready, the lasagne should be lightly browned on top

Cut into portions

- Cut the lasagne into portions

Serve

- Serve with a side salad and crusty bread

image taken from video

Macaroni Cheese Bake

Oven-baked pasta with basil and garlic, coated with a creamy cheese sauce and topped with fresh breadcrumbs and Parmesan for extra crunch.

RATING  

Ingredients

- 1 slice white bread (to make breadcrumbs)
- 340g macaroni
- 1 clove of garlic
- 2 large handfuls fresh basil (about 10g)
- salt and black pepper
- 3 handfuls freshly grated Parmesan cheese (about 50g)

For the cheese sauce

- 40g butter
- 40g plain flour
- 500ml semi-skimmed milk
- 50g gruyere cheese (grated)
- salt and white pepper

Utensils

- bread/serrated knife
- chopping board
- food processor
- medium saucepan
- chopping knife
- seive or colander
- slotted spoon
- small saucepan
- wooden spoon
- cheese grater
- large oven dish
- serving spoon

A typical serving contains (based on the max. number of people this recipe serves):

Calories	Sugar	Fat	Saturates	Salt
295	4.0g	10g	6.0g	0.5g
17%	4.5%	14%	30%	11%

of a child's guideline daily amount

Prepare the ingredients

Remove the crusts from the bread

- To make the breadcrumbs, first cut the crusts off the bread

Chop it into chunks

- Chop the bread into chunks

Put the bread in the blender

- Put the chunks of bread in the food processor and blend for about 30 seconds to make the breadcrumbs

Cook the macaroni

- Put a medium saucepan of water on to boil and add a pinch of salt
- When the water is boiling, add the macaroni and give it a stir to stop it sticking together
- The macaroni should take about 15 minutes to cook

Peel the garlic

- Crush the garlic under your knife to remove the skin

Chop it finely

- Chop the garlic finely

Pick the basil leaves

- Pick the basil leaves from the stem

Chop the basil

- Roughly chop the basil

Drain the macaroni

- When cooked, remove the macaroni with a slotted spoon and drain through a sieve

Step 2 Make the cheese sauce

Melt the butter in a saucepan

- Put a small saucepan on a medium heat and add the 40g of butter

Add the flour and mix to a paste

- When the butter has melted and is foaming, add the flour and mix vigorously with a wooden spoon until it forms a paste

Then add a little milk

- Then add the cold milk, a little at a time, mixing as you go

Mix until combined

- Make sure the milk is completely combined before adding any more
- You want to beat out the lumps in the sauce, so mix vigorously

Use all of the milk

- Each time, when the milk has mixed with the sauce, add a bit more milk and mix well again
- Keep going until all the milk is used

It should go smooth and creamy

- When all the milk is used, the sauce should go smooth and creamy

Bring to the boil and add cheese

- Bring the sauce to the boil, stirring continuously
- Then add the grated cheese

Stir until the cheese has melted

- Continue to stir the sauce constantly to melt the cheese

Season

- Season with salt and ground white pepper, and mix in

That's it!

- Just let it simmer gently for about 5 minutes, stirring occasionally so it doesn't stick to the bottom
- Turn off the heat

Make & cook the bake

Butter a large oven dish

- Lightly butter a large oven dish
- This will help stop the pasta sticking and will make it easier to wash!

Add the macaroni

- Add the drained pasta to the oven dish

Break it up

- Break the macaroni up if it's stuck together

Add the garlic

- Sprinkle the chopped garlic over the top

Add the basil

- Then add the chopped basil

Season

- Season with salt and black pepper

Spoon on the cheese sauce

- Spoon the cheese sauce over the macaroni

Mix together well

- Mix the cheese sauce into the macaroni so it is totally covered

Cover with breadcrumbs

- Sprinkle the breadcrumbs over the top of the bake

Then the grated Parmesan

- Sprinkle the Parmesan over to finish

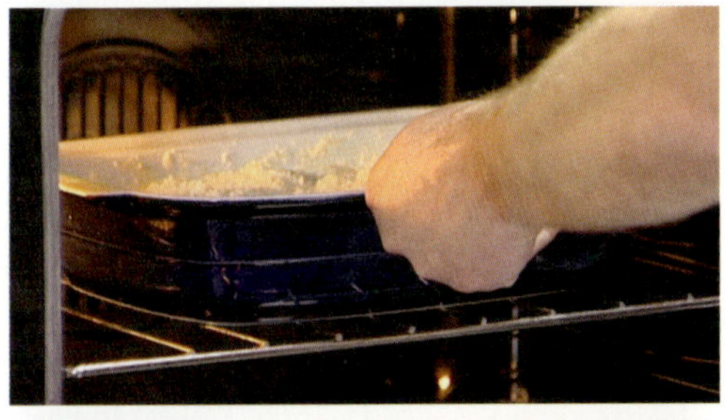

Put the dish in the oven

- Bake in a pre-heated oven at 180°C (350°F or gas mark 4) for 15–20minutes

It should be golden brown on top

- When it's cooked, it should be lightly browned and crispy on the top

That's it!

- The bake should still be creamy on the inside

Serve and enjoy!

image taken from video

Spag Bol

The classic Italian staple – made even easier!

PREP TIME **15** MINUTES | COOK TIME **20** MINUTES | SERVES **4** PEOPLE

RATING   

Ingredients

- 2 medium onions
- 1 large or 2 small cloves of garlic
- 2 tablespoons olive oil
- 450g lean minced beef
- 1 tablespoon tomato purée
- 1 x 400g can chopped tomatoes
- 150ml beef stock
- a few drops of Worcestershire sauce
- 1 teaspoon fresh thyme leaves (plus extra for serving)
- salt and freshly ground black pepper
- 300g dried spaghetti
- Parmesan cheese (for serving)

Utensils

- small chopping knife
- chopping board
- chopping knife
- 2 medium saucepans
- wooden spoon
- slotted spoon
- sieve or colander
- tongs
- ladle

A typical serving contains (based on the max. number of people this recipe serves):

Calories	Sugar	Fat	Saturates	Salt
561	9g	20g	6g	0.6g
31%	10%	28%	30%	15%

of a child's guideline daily amount

Make the bolognaise sauce

Peel the onions

- First, peel the onions

Slice horizontally

- Carefully slice the onion horizontally

Slice along the core

- Then slice the onion along the core – but not all the way to the end – this will hold it together

Turn through 90° and dice finely

Peel the garlic

- Crush the garlic under your knife to remove the skin

Chop finely

- Chop the garlic finely

Put it in a pan

- Put a medium saucepan on a medium heat and cover the bottom with olive oil
- Add the chopped onion and garlic and fry for 2–3 minutes

Add the mince and break it up

- Then add the minced beef to the pan and break it up using a wooden spoon – this will stop it sticking together

Fry

- Fry until it has browned, or 'sealed' all over

Add tomato purée and mix

- When the mince is brown, add the tomato purée and mix it in

Add the chopped tomatoes

- Add the tin of chopped tomatoes

Mix together well

- Stir the pan well to coat the beef in the tomatoes

Add the beef stock

- Add the beef stock to the pan

Add the Worcestershire sauce

- Mix it together and add the Worcestershire sauce

Mix

- Mix the bolognaise together well

Add the thyme leaves

- Pick the leaves from the fresh thyme and add them to the pan
- Stir the thyme into the sauce

Season

- Season with salt and pepper

Simmer

- Bring the bolognaise to the boil and simmer with the lid on for about 15–20 minutes to cook the beef

Step 2 Cook the spaghetti & serve

Add oil to boiling, salted water

- Bring a pan of water to the boil
- Add a pinch of salt and add a little olive oil

Add the spaghetti

- When the water is boiling, add the spaghetti and cook for about 10–15 minutes

Stir occasionally

- Keep stirring it occasionally so it doesn't stick together

Test the spaghetti is cooked

- Squeeze a strand of spaghetti between your fingers – if it breaks easily, it's cooked

Drain the spaghetti

- When the pasta is cooked, drain it through a colander or sieve

Put the spaghetti in a bowl

- Put the spaghetti in a bowl and pour over a little olive oil – this will help to stop it sticking together

Coat the spaghetti in oil

- Coat the spaghetti in the oil using the tongs

Stir the bolognaise sauce

- Give the sauce one last stir before you serve
- Turn off the heat

Put the spaghetti on the plate

- Use the tongs to put the spaghetti on the plates

Serve

- Spoon the bolognaise sauce on top
- Serve with a little Parmesan cheese sprinkled over the top and a sprig of thyme

image taken from video

Fusilli Carbonara

Classic Italian energy burst with sugar snaps, bacon and garlic.

PREP TIME **15** MINUTES

COOK TIME **20** MINUTES

SERVES **4–6** PEOPLE

RATING

Ingredients

- 100g sugar snaps
- 1 clove garlic
- 6 rashers smoked streaky bacon
- 1 egg
- olive oil and salt to cook the pasta
- 150ml single cream
- 300g dried fusilli
  (we have used quick-cook fusilli)
- 2 handfuls freshly grated Parmesan cheese
- salt and freshly ground black pepper

Utensils

- chopping knife
- chopping board
- small mixing bowl
- fork
- medium saucepan
- large frying pan
- wooden spoon
- sieve or colander
- slotted spoon

A typical serving contains (based on the max. number of people this recipe serves):

Calories	Sugar	Fat	Saturates	Salt
338	2.0g	15g	6.5g	0.9g
19%	2%	21%	32%	22%

of a child's guideline daily amount

Step 1 Prepare

Slice the sugar snaps finely

- First, put a half-filled pan of water on to boil
- Finely slice the sugar snaps and put them to one side

Peel the garlic

- Crush the garlic under your knife to remove the skin

Chop it finely

- Chop the garlic finely and put it to one side

Slice the bacon

- Cut the bacon into fine strips and put that to one side as well

Crack the egg

- Crack the egg into a small bowl

Beat the egg

- Beat the egg with a fork

Cook

Add oil to the boiling, salted water

- Add a pinch of salt and a little olive oil to the boiling water in the pan

Add the pasta

- Add the fusilli and cook for a few minutes – we have used quick-cook pasta, so it will only take a few minutes to cook
- Check the packet instructions before you start

Put the garlic in the frying pan

- Put a frying pan on a medium heat and add the olive oil
- Add the garlic and fry for a minute

Add the bacon

- Add the bacon and cook for another couple of minutes

Add the sugar snaps

- Add the sugar snaps
- Keep it continually moving to cook the bacon through

The pasta is cooked

- The pasta should be 'al dente', which means firm to bite when its cooked

Drain the pasta

- Drain the pasta through a sieve

Add to the frying pan

- Add the pasta to the frying pan with the bacon and sugar snaps

Mix in

- Mix it together

Add the single cream

- Add the single cream to the pan

Mix

- Mix it in to coat all of the pasta

Add the Parmesan

- Add the Parmesan and mix it in

Add the egg

- Add the beaten egg – don't cook the egg for any longer than 2–3 minutes or it will scramble

Season

- Add a small pinch of salt and some black pepper

That's it!

- That's it!
- Turn off the heat

Serve

- Serve and enjoy!

image taken from video

Hi-Five Pasta

Get your 5-a-day here. Fresh tagliatelle with 5 varieties of vegetables cunningly hidden in a tomato sauce.

PREP TIME **10** MINUTES | COOK TIME **20** MINUTES | SERVES **4** PEOPLE

RATING  

Ingredients

- 2 cloves of garlic
- 30ml olive oil
- 8 button mushrooms
- 1 medium carrot
- ½ a medium courgette
- ½ a medium aubergine (or ¼ of a large one)
- 4 ripe tomatoes
- 1 tablespoon balsamic vinegar
- 1 x 400g tin plum tomatoes
- 4 tablespoons double cream
- 200g half fat mozzarella or mascarpone
- salt and pepper
- olive oil and salt to cook the pasta
- 450g fresh tagliatelle
- handful grated Parmesan cheese

Utensils

- chopping knife
- chopping board
- frying pan with lid
- small chopping knife
- wooden spoon
- vetetable peeler
- medium saucepan
- sieve
- medium mixing bowl
- carving fork (optional)

A typical serving contains (based on the max. number of people this recipe serves):

Calories	Sugar	Fat	Saturates	Salt
565	12g	19g	4.0g	0.3g
31%	14%	27%	20%	7.5%

of a child's guideline daily amount

Make the sauce

Peel the garlic

- First, prepare the garlic – crush it under your knife to remove the skin

Chop it finely

- Chop the garlic finely

Put the oil in the frying pan

- Put a frying pan on a medium heat and add a little olive oil

Add the garlic and fry

- Fry the chopped garlic in the oil for a couple of minutes

Slice the mushrooms

- Slice the mushrooms finely

Add them to the pan and stir

- Add the mushrooms to the pan and stir them while they cook

Peel the carrot

- Peel the carrot with a vegetable peeler

Remove the ends

- Remove the ends of the carrot

Give the mushrooms a quick stir

- Give the mushrooms a quick stir in the pan so that they don't burn

Peel strips from the carrot

- Discard the carrot skin then, using the peeler again, peel ribbons from the carrot
- Peel all the way down to the core

Add the carrot to the pan and stir

- Add the carrot ribbons to the pan along with the garlic and mushrooms and stir again

Prepare the courgette

- Remove the end of the ½ courgette

Split in half lengthways

- Split the courgette in half along its length

Slice it finely, at an angle

- Slice the courgette finely, at an angle

Add to the pan and stir

- Add the courgette to the pan and stir

Cut the ½ aubergine in two

- Lay the ½ aubergine flat and cut it in two

Slice it thinly

- Cut the aubergine into thin slices

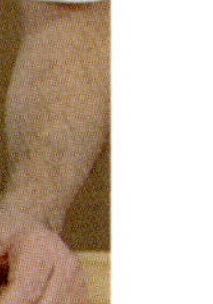

Put it in the pan and stir

- Add the aubergine to the pan and stir it in

Prepare the tomatoes

- Halve, then quarter the tomatoes

Chop them into chunks

- Roughly chop the tomatoes into small chunks

Stir occasionally

- Make sure you stir the pan every so often

Add the tomatoes and stir

- Add the tomatoes to the pan and stir them in

Put the lid on to cook through

- Put the lid on the pan to let the vegetables cook through for a couple of minutes and sweat down

Add the balsamic vinegar

- After a couple of minutes, add the balsamic vinegar

Add the chopped tomatoes and stir

- Then add the tin of chopped tomatoes and mix everything together

Put the lid on and bring to the boil

- Put the lid on and bring the pan to the boil
- Cook for 1–2 minutes

Add the double cream

- Add the double cream, mix it in

Mix in and bring to the boil

- Bring the pan to the boil and then simmer

Crumble the mozzarella

- After about a minute of cooking, crumble the mozzarella into the sauce

Stir the cheese in and put the lid on

- Stir the cheese in, then put the lid back on and let it melt

Stir occasionally until melted

- Stir the sauce occasionally to make sure the cheese has melted

Season

- When the cheese has melted, season with salt and pepper
- That's it!
- Turn off the heat

Step 2 Cook the pasta & serve

Add oil to boiling, salted water

- We are using fresh tagliatelli, so it will only take a couple of minutes to cook
- Bring a pan of water to the boil on a medium heat
- Add a little olive oil and salt

Add the pasta

- Put the fresh pasta into the boiling water and cook for 2–3 minutes until 'al dente', or firm to the bite

Drain the pasta

- Drain the pasta through a sieve
- Turn off the heat

Add some oil to the pasta

- Add a little olive oil to stop the pasta sticking together and carefully mix it through

Serve the sauce

- Give the pasta sauce a stir and turn off the heat when cooked
- Spoon some of the sauce on the plate or bowl

Twist the pasta

- You can use a carving fork to twirl the pasta around to make a bundle
- Alternatively you can mix the pasta and sauce together and serve in a bowl

Slide the pasta onto the sauce

- Carefully slide the pasta off the fork onto the top of the sauce

Top with Parmesan to finish

- Sprinkle with Parmesan cheese to finish

image taken from video

Beef Stew and Dumplings

A British winter warmer with lean braising steak, lots of vegetables and bacon-and-onion-flavoured dumplings.

PREP TIME 30 MINUTES | COOK TIME $1\frac{3}{4}$ HOURS | SERVES 4–6 PEOPLE

RATING

Ingredients

- 1 clove of garlic
- 2 large onions
- 25g unsalted butter
- 1 tablespoon olive oil
- 600g braising steak
- 1 tablespoon plain flour
- 1 tablespoon tomato purée
- 1 litre of beef stock
- 1 bay leaf
- salt and pepper
- 2 pinches of dried thyme (or 2 sprigs of fresh)
- some fresh parsley for serving
- 3 carrots
- 3 sticks of celery
- 2 large potatoes
- 200g button mushrooms

For the dumplings
- 1 onion
- 4 rashers smoked bacon
- ½ tablespoon olive oil
- 2 teaspoons baking powder
- 250g plain flour (plus extra for dusting/making the dumplings)
- 1 teaspoon dried, chopped parsley
- 100g fresh or dried beef suet
- 150ml water

Utensils

- large chopping knife
- chopping board
- large pot or saucepan with lid
- wooden spoon
- vegetable peeler
- small chopping knife
- large mixing bowl
- frying pan
- measuring jug
- ladle

A typical serving contains (based on the max. number of people this recipe serves):

Calories	Sugar	Fat	Saturates	Salt
659	9g	37g	15g	2.1g
37%	10%	53%	75%	52%

of a child's guideline daily amount

Make the stew base

Peel the garlic

- Crush the garlic under your knife to remove the skin

Chop it finely

- Chop the garlic finely

Peel the onion

- Peel the onion and chop it in half

Chop it into chunks

- Chop the onion into chunks

Put the butter and oil in the pan

- Put a large pot or saucepan on a medium heat
- Add the 25g butter and the tablespoon of olive oil

Add the garlic and onion

- When the butter is foaming, add the garlic and onion and fry for about 5 minutes

Fry for a few minutes

- Fry until the onion turns slightly brown

Meanwhile, prepare the steak

- Take the braising steak and remove any fat and sinew

Dice the steak

- Cut the steaks into large chunks, making sure to remove any large pieces of fat you might have missed

Add the diced steak to the pan

- When the onions have slightly browned, add the beef to the pot

Cook until sealed

- Cook the steak until it's browned, or 'sealed'
- Turn up the heat slightly if you need to – this will help seal it faster

Then add the flour and mix in

- When it has sealed, add the plain flour to the beef and onions in the pot
- This will help absorb some of the fat so it's not too greasy – it will also help to thicken the gravy

Add the tomato purée

- Next, add the tomato purée to the pot

Mix it in until the beef is coated

- Mix the tomato purée in until the beef is coated

Add half of the beef stock

- Now add half of the beef stock

Mix thoroughly to combine

- Mix the pot thoroughly to combine the stock with the other ingredients

Then add the remaining stock

- Add the remaining stock to the pan

Add the bay leaf and thyme

- Now add the thyme and the bay leaf

Give it a stir and bring to the boil

- Stir the pot and bring it to the boil

Put the lid on and simmer

- Put the lid on and simmer for 20 minutes
- You will need to cook the stew for 2 hours in total

Step 2 Prepare the vegetables

Peel the carrots

- While the stew is simmering, you can prepare the rest of the vegetables that will go in the stew
- Peel the carrots with a vegetable peeler and discard the skins

Halve them lengthways

- Remove the ends and then halve the carrots lengthways

Slice them diagonally

- Slice the carrots diagonally

Remove the ends of the celery

- Cut the ends off the celery sticks and discard

Slice it diagonally

- Slice the celery diagonally, in the same way as the carrots

Peel the potatoes

- Peel the potatoes with the peeler

Chop them into chunks

- Chop them into large chunks
- Put them in a bowl of clean water until you need them

Wipe any dirt from the mushrooms

- Keep the button mushrooms whole
- Give them a quick wipe to remove any dirt
- If they are very dirty you will need to wash them more thoroughly

Cut any large ones in half

- Cut any large mushrooms in half

Add the veg & make the dumplings

Add the carrots to the stew

- After the stew has simmered for 20 minutes, add the carrots

Start on the dumplings

- Now you can start on the dumplings
- First, peel the onion

Slice the onion horizontally

- Slice the onion horizontally with your hand flat on the top

Slice it along the core

- Then slice the onion along the core, but not all the way to the end – this will hold it togther

Turn it through 90° and dice finely

Cut the bacon slices in half

- Cut the bacon slices in half

Cut them into thin strips

- Then cut the bacon into thin strips

Dice the bacon finely

- Dice the bacon as finely as possible

Add the onion to the pan

- Put a frying pan on a medium heat with the ½ tablespoon of olive oil
- Add the onions to the frying pan and fry them gently (you don't want them to go brown!)

Add the bacon

- When the onions are lightly fried, add the bacon to the frying pan as well
- Stir-fry the bacon and onions for 2–3 minutes, until the bacon is cooked

Take the pan off the heat

- When the bacon is cooked, take the pan off the heat

Add the celery to the stew

- After the carrots have cooked for 10 minutes, add the celery to the stew

Put baking powder/flour in a bowl

- Add the baking powder to the flour and mix them together in a mixing bowl

Add the dried parsley

- Add the dried parsley and mix it in

Add the beef suet and mix

- Add the beef suet and mix this in as well

Add the bacon and the onions

- Finally, add the bacon and onions to the bowl

Mix well, then add the water

- Mix everything together well with a wooden spoon
- Add the 150ml water and mix together thoroughly

Mix until you have a sticky dough

- Mix until you have a thick, sticky dumpling dough

Season with salt and pepper

Add the potatoes to the stew

- 20 minutes after adding the celery to the stew, add the potatoes

Flour a large plate or bowl

- Sprinkle flour on a large plate or bowl

Roll the dumplings into balls

- Roll the dumpling mix into balls in your hands
- They should each be about the size of a golf ball
- Make sure you flour your hands so that the dough doesn't stick to them

The mixture should make about 12

- Make as many dumplings as you can with the mix – we managed 12

Add the mushrooms to the stew

- 5 minutes after adding the potatoes, add the mushrooms to the stew

Season the stew

- Season the stew with salt and pepper and mix in

Put the stew in a large oven dish

- Ladle the stew into a large oven dish
- Turn off the heat

Add the dumplings

- Carefully float the dumplings on the top

Put the stew in the oven

- Cook in the oven at 180°C (350°F or gas mark 4 for 20 minutes)
- The dumplings will puff up while they are cooking

Serve

Pick the parsley

- Pick the parsley leaves from the stem

Chop it finely

- Chop the parsley finely and put it to one side

Remove the stew

- Remove the stew from the oven – the dumplings will have puffed up quite a lot!
- Turn off the oven

Test the dumplings are cooked

- To test whether the dumplings are cooked, cut into one – there should be no doughy mix in the middle

Serve

- Ladle the stew into bowls to serve
- Serve a few dumplings in the bowls with the stew
- Sprinkle with the chopped parsley to finish

Image taken from video

Haddock and Prawn Smokies

Poached haddock and king prawns in a creamy cheese sauce, served in individual pots with a tangy watercress salad. If you want a stronger flavour, use the milk you used to cook the fish in to make the cheese sauce!

PREP TIME 15 MINUTES | COOK TIME 30 MINUTES | SERVES 4 PEOPLE

RATING     

Ingredients

- 300g smoked haddock (you can also use smoked cod)
- 300ml semi-skimmed milk (or enough to cover the fish when cooking)
- 1 bay leaf
- 300g king prawns
- a handful of grated Parmesan

For the cheese sauce
- 40g butter
- 40g plain flour
- 500ml semi-skimmed milk
- 50g gruyere cheese (grated)
- salt and ground white pepper

For the salad
- 30ml olive oil
- 10ml balsamic vinegar
- 1 x 110g bag watercress, spinach and rocket salad

Utensils

- large oven dish
- tin foil
- medium saucepan
- wooden spoon
- fork
- tablespoon
- 2 medium mixing bowls
- small pots to cook the smokies in
- baking tray
- jam jar (with lid)

A typical serving contains (based on the max. number of people this recipe serves):

Calories	Sugar	Fat	Saturates	Salt
461	7.0g	26g	12g	2.1g
26%	8%	37%	60%	52%

of a child's guideline daily amount

Poach the fish

Put the haddock in an oven dish

- Put the haddock in a large oven dish

Cover with milk

- Pour over enough milk to cover the fish

Add a bay leaf

- Add a bay leaf to the milk.

Cover the dish in tin foil

- Cover the oven dish in tin foil

Put it in the oven

- Put it in the oven, pre-heated to 180°C (350°F or gas mark 4) for 15 minutes to poach the fish
- Meanwhile, if you have shell-on prawns you can shell them now

Making the cheese sauce

Melt the butter in a saucepan

- Put a small saucepan on a medium heat and add the 40g of butter

When foaming, add the flour

- When the butter has melted and is foaming, add the flour

Mix to a paste

- Mix vigorously with a wooden spoon until it forms a paste

Add a little milk

- Then add the cold milk, a little at a time, mixing as you go

Mix until combined

- Make sure the milk is completely combined before you add any more

Keep adding milk and mixing

- Each time the milk has mixed with the sauce, add a little more and mix well again

It should be smooth and creamy

- You want to beat out the lumps in the sauce, so keep stirring!
- Keep going until all the milk is used and the mix is smooth and creamy

Bring to the boil

- When all the milk is used, bring the pan to the boil, stirring continuously

Add the cheese

- Add the grated cheese to the sauce and stir constantly to melt it

Season with salt and white pepper

- Season with salt and ground white pepper

Stir until thick and creamy

- Let it simmer gently for about 5 minutes, stirring occasionally so it doesn't stick to the bottom
- It should go thick and creamy

Making the smokies

Take the fish out of the oven

- When the haddock is cooked, take it out of the oven and carefully remove the tin foil

Check it's cooked

- Check it's cooked by cutting in to it
- The flesh should be firm and opaque

Drain the fish

- Drain the fish and put it on a plate

Flake the fish

- Carefully flake the fish from the skin, making sure to remove all the bones as you go

Put the fish in a mixing bowl

- Then put the flaked fish in a mixing bowl

Add the prawns

- Add the prawns to the haddock

Mix them together

- Gently mix them together

Season

- Season with pepper

Ladle over the cheese sauce

- Add the cheese sauce to the haddock and prawns in the bowl

Gently mix together

- Mix the fish and sauce together gently so as not to break up the haddock too much

Spoon into pots

- Put the small pots on a baking tray
- Divide the smokie mix evenly between the pots

Sprinkle Parmesan on top

- Sprinkle the tops of the pots with grated Parmesan cheese

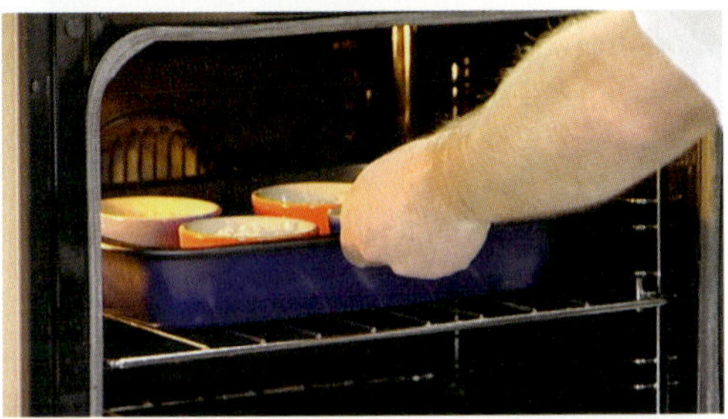

Put them in the oven

- Put them in an oven, pre-heated at 180°C (350°F or gas mark 4) for 10 minutes

Remove the smokies from the oven

- After 10 minutes, remove the smokies from the oven

Should be browned on top

- The smokies will be lightly browned on the top when they are cooked
- Turn off the oven

Step 4 Make the salad & serve

Make the dressing

- Put the watercress, spinach and rocket salad in a bowl
- Put the olive oil into a jam jar or pot that has a lid

Add the balsamic vinegar

- Add the balsamic vinegar to the jar

Put the lid on the jar and shake

- Put the lid on and shake vigorously to combine the oil and vinegar
- That's the dressing finished!

Drizzle over the salad

- Put the salad in a bowl and drizzle over the dressing just before you serve

Toss the salad

- Mix the salad and dressing together thoroughly

Season

- Season with salt and pepper

Serve

- Serve a handful of the salad on the plate with the smokie pots

image taken from video

Tomato and Vegetable Noodles

A healthy noodle snack with fresh tomatoes, noodles and vegetable broth. Great served with soy sauce.

PREP TIME **10** MINUTES | COOK TIME **15** MINUTES | SERVES **4** PEOPLE

RATING 

Ingredients

- 3 spring onions
- 2 tablespoons sesame oil
- ½ a red onion
- 1 pak choi
- 4 large vine or plum tomatoes
- 600ml vegetable stock
- salt and pepper
- water to cook the noodles
- 230g dried medium egg noodles
- 1 tablespoon soy sauce (plus more to serve)

Utensils

- chopping board
- chopping knife
- frying pan
- wooden spoon
- small chopping knife
- measuring jug
- medium saucepan
- sieve or colander
- fork
- ladle
- tongs
- chopsticks (optional!)

A typical serving contains (based on the max. number of people this recipe serves):

Calories	Sugar	Fat	Saturates	Salt
314	6.0g	11g	2.0g	1.0g
17%	7%	16%	10%	25%

of a child's guideline daily amount

Stir-fry

Slice the end of the spring onions

- Finely slice the green ends of the spring onions and put them to one side

Chop the remaining part into 3

- Chop the light end of the spring onion into 3 pieces

Put the oil in the pan

- Put the sesame oil in a frying pan and, when hot, add the light-coloured spring onion ends

Peel the ½ red onion

Slice it finely

- Slice the red onion finely

Add the onions

- Add the onions to the pan and stir-fry

Cut the pak choi into quarters

- Quarter the pak choi

Remove the core

- Remove the core from each quarter
- Cut any large pieces in half

Add to the pan and stir-fry

- Add the pak choi to the pan and stir-fry for 1–2 minutes

Prepare the tomatoes

- Chop the tomatoes into quarters

Cut out the seeds

- Carefully cut the seeds out of the tomato quarters

Cut into strips

- Then cut the tomato flesh into strips

Add them to the pan and stir-fry

- Add the tomatoes to the pan and stir for 1–2 minutes

Add the vegetable stock

- Then add the stock

Simmer

- Bring the stock to the boil, stirring it occasionally
- Simmer for 3–5 minutes – not too long though, as the tomatoes may begin to break up

Cook the noodles

Cook the noodles

- Bring a pan of slightly-salted water to the boil
- When the water is boiling, add the noodles, bring the water back to the boil and then cook for 2 minutes

Check the stir-fry

- Stir the pan occasionally

Drain the noodles

- Drain the noodles when cooked

Add the noodles to the frying pan

- Then add the noodles to the frying pan and carefully mix them together with the vegetables

Add the soy sauce

- Add the soy sauce to the pan

Season

- Season with salt and pepper
- Simmer for another couple of minutes, and that's it!
- Turn off the heat

Serve

- Serve sprinkled with a few of the chopped green spring onion ends

image taken from video

Chicken and Mushroom Noodles

A healthy noodle snack with fresh chicken breast, mushrooms, noodles and chicken broth, topped with spring onion.

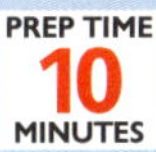

Ingredients

- 2 large onions
- 2 tablespoons sesame oil
- 3 spring onions
- 100g oyster mushrooms
- teaspoon chopped fresh parsley
- 2 chicken breasts
- 600ml chicken stock
- salt and pepper
- water to cook the noodles
- 230g dried egg noodles
- soy sauce to serve

Utensils

- chopping knife
- small chopping knife
- chopping board
- frying pan
- wooden spoon
- measuring jug
- medium saucepan
- seive or colander
- tongs
- chopsticks (optional!)

A typical serving contains (based on the max. number of people this recipe serves):

Calories	Sugar	Fat	Saturates	Salt
424	4.0g	15g	4.0g	1.1g
23%	5%	21%	20%	27%

of a child's guideline daily amount

Stir-fry

Peel the onions

- Peel the onions

Add the oil to the pan

- Add the sesame oil to the frying pan on a medium heat

Slice the onions

- Slice the onions into fine strips

Add the onions to the pan

- Put the onions in the pan and fry

Slice the spring onions

- Slice the spring onions and put them to one side

Slice the mushrooms

- Roughly slice the oyster mushrooms into strips

Add them to the pan

- Add them to the pan with the onions and stir-fry for 2–3 minutes

Pick the parsley leaves

- Pick the parsley leaves from the stem

Chop them finely

- Chop them finely, then put them to one side

Slice the chicken breast

- Slice the chicken breast into fine strips

Halve any large pieces

- If the chicken breast is large you can cut it down the middle before you slice them

Slice

- Then slice the chicken finely

Add the chicken to the pan

- Add the sliced chicken to the pan and stir-fry until it is sealed (browned all over)

Add the stock

- When the chicken is sealed, add the stock to the pan, bring to the boil and simmer

Add the parsley

- When simmering, add the chopped parsley

Season

- Season with salt and pepper

Mix and simmer

- Mix together and simmer while you cook the noodles

Step 2

Cook the noodles & serve

Add the noodles to a pan

- Bring a pan of slightly salted water to the boil
- When the water in the saucepan comes to the boil, add the dried egg noodles
- Bring the water back to the boil and cook for 2 minutes

Drain and add to the pan

- As soon as the noodles are cooked, drain them and add them to the frying pan as well

Mix

- Stir them in to mix all the ingredients together

Add the spring onion

- Add the finely chopped spring onion
- Cook for another minute or two, then turn off the heat

Serve

- Serve the noodles in a bowl or pot

Image taken from video

BBQ Beef Noodles

A healthy noodle snack with fresh beef stock, hoisin sauce and beef broth.

PREP TIME	COOK TIME	SERVES
10 MINUTES	15 MINUTES	4 PEOPLE

RATING   

Ingredients

- 1 red onion
- 2 tablespoons sesame oil
- 3 spring onions
- 230g beef sirloin
- 40ml hoisin barbeque sauce
- 1 tablespoon reduced sodium soy sauce (and a little more for serving)
- 600ml beef stock
- 230g dried medium egg noodles

Utensils

- chopping board
- chopping knife
- frying pan
- wooden spoon
- measuring jug
- medium saucepan
- chopsticks (optional!)
- tongs

A typical serving contains (based on the max. number of people this recipe serves):

Calories	Sugar	Fat	Saturates	Salt
407	3.0g	18g	3.5g	2.5g
23%	3%	26%	17%	62%

of a child's guideline daily amount

Stir-fry

Peel the red onion

- Peel the red onion

Add the oil to the pan

- Put a frying pan on a medium heat and add the sesame oil

Slice the onion

- Halve the red onion
- Then slice it finely

Add it to the frying pan

- When the pan is hot, add the sliced red onion to the pan

Slice the spring onions

- Slice the spring onions, and put them to one side

Give the onions a stir

- Give the onions a stir

Remove any sinew and fat

- Remove any sinew and fat from the steaks

Slice the steak thinly

- Slice the steak as thinly as you can

Add it to the pan and stir-fry

- Add the beef to the pan and stir-fry

Fry until sealed

- Fry the beef until it is sealed (browned all over)

Then add the hoisin sauce

- Add the hoisin sauce

Stir-fry until coated

- Stir-fry the beef until it is completely coated in the hoisin sauce

Mix in the soy sauce

- Add the soy sauce and mix it in

Add the stock

- Next add the beef stock to the frying pan and bring it to the boil

Simmer

- Let it simmer for a minute or two, stirring occasionally while you cook the noodles

Step 2

Cook the noodles & serve

Add the noodles to a pan

- Bring a pan of water to the boil
- When the water is boiling, add the noodles
- Bring the water back to the boil and cook the noodles for 2 minutes

Drain the noodles when cooked

- When the noodles are cooked, drain them

Add the noodles to the frying pan

- Add the noodles to the frying pan with the beef

Mix together

- Stir the mix together
- You can use chopsticks to do this

Add the spring onion

- Add the spring onions to the pan just before serving

Mix

- Mix the spring onion into the noodles
- Turn off the heat

Serve

- Serve in small bowls or pots

image taken from video

Chicken Fajitas

Mexican food made easy! Fresh chicken breast with red pepper, chilli, tomatoes, paprika and sour cream.

PREP TIME 10 MINUTES | COOK TIME 10 MINUTES | SERVES 4 PEOPLE | RATING  

Ingredients

- 1 clove of garlic
- ½ red onion
- ½ red pepper
- ¼ red chilli
- 1 chicken breast
- 1 tablespoon olive oil
- 1 teaspoon dried or fresh oregano
- ½ a teaspoon of paprika
- salt and pepper
- 200g chopped tomatoes (½ a 400g can)
- ¼ medium iceberg lettuce
- 4 small flour tortillas
- 4 tablespoons sour cream

- parsley for decoration

Utensils

- chopping knife
- chopping board
- small chopping knife
- frying pan
- wooden spoon

A typical serving contains (based on the max. number of people this recipe serves):

Calories	Sugar	Fat	Saturates	Salt
274	4.0g	1.0g	5.0g	0.8g
15%	5%	16%	25%	20%

of a child's guideline daily amount

Prepare the chicken & vegetables

Peel the garlic

- Crush the garlic under your knife or your hand to remove the skin

Chop finely

- Finely chop the garlic

Prepare the onion

- Chop the red onion in half
- Peel half of the onion

Slice it finely

- Slice the ½ onion finely

Remove the core from the pepper

- Halve the red pepper and pull out the core

Slice into thin strips

- Slice half of the pepper into strips

Split the chilli lengthways

- Split the chilli in half lengthways

Remove the stalk

- Remove the green stalk from the chilli
- We will only use half of the chilli

Split the half

- Split the half into half again

Scrape out the seeds

- Scrape the seeds out from the chilli (the seeds are the hottest part!)
- We only need a quarter of the chilli, so discard the remaining quarter

Slice into fine strips

- Slice the quarter chilli into fine strips

Cut the chicken breast in half

- Cut the chicken breast in half at an angle – this will help you slice it thinly

Slice finely

- Slice the chicken into fine strips

Step 2 Cook the fajitas

Put the olive oil in the pan

- Put the olive oil in a frying pan on a medium heat

Add the garlic, onion and chilli

- Add the garlic, onion and chilli

Stir-fry

- Stir-fry the garlic, onion and chilli for a minute or two

Add the red pepper

- Now add the red pepper and fry for another minute

Add the chicken

- Add the chicken and stir-fry again until the chicken is lightly browned

Add the oregano and paprika

- Next add the oregano and paprika and stir-fry to coat the chicken

Season

- Season with salt and pepper

Add the tomatoes

- Add the chopped tomatoes and stir

Simmer

- Simmer for 2 minutes
- After 2 minutes, it's ready, so turn off the heat

Wrap & serve

Core the lettuce

- Remove the core from the lettuce

Shred the lettuce finely

- Shred the lettuce finely and put it to one side

Warm the tortillas

- You may need to warm the tortillas in the microwave (this will make them softer so they are less likely to split when you wrap them up)
- Warm them for about 20 seconds, or according to the instructions on the packet

Spoon the chicken onto the tortilla

- Spoon the chicken along the centre of each wrap
- Make sure you leave space at the bottom

Add the lettuce

- Top with the shredded lettuce

Add the sour cream

- Add a dollop of sour cream

Fold the bottom of the tortilla up

- To wrap the fajitas, first fold the bottom of the tortilla up, leaving it open at one end
- This will stop anything falling out of the bottom when you eat it!

Wrap one side over

- Wrap one side over the top of the chicken

Wrap second side

- Then wrap the second side round tightly

Hold together with a sandwich stick

- Here we have used sandwich sticks to hold the fajitas together which are safer than cocktail sticks

Serve

- Wrap all the fajitas and serve
- Why not let your kids wrap them!

Image taken from video

Chilli Con Carne

with Cheesy Corn Chips

Sweet chilli sauce adds a new dimension to this classic Mexican chilli. Served with cheese-coated corn chips for an authentic taste. The sour cream dampens the spiciness.

PREP TIME **10** MINUTES | COOK TIME **25** MINUTES | SERVES **4** PEOPLE | RATING   

Ingredients

For the chilli

- 2 cloves of garlic
- salt and pepper
- 1½ medium onions
- 2 tablespoons olive oil
- 450g lean minced beef
- 1 teaspoon of paprika
- 1 tablespoon tomato purée
- 1 x 400g can chopped tomatoes
- 150ml beef stock
- 2 teaspoons sweet chilli sauce
- a few drops of Worcestershire sauce
- 300g can kidney beans

For the cheesy corn chips (optional)

- 240g packet corn chips
- 120g grated mild cheddar cheese
- 120g sour cream

- a sprig of parsley to serve

Utensils

- chopping knife
- chopping board
- small chopping knife
- medium saucepan
- wooden spoon
- jug
- large baking tray
- ladle
- spatula

A typical serving contains (based on the max. number of people this recipe serves):

Calories	Sugar	Fat	Saturates	Salt
337	8.0g	18g	6.0g	1.0g
19%	9%	26%	30%	25%

of a child's guideline daily amount

Make the chilli

Peel the garlic

- Crush the garlic under your knife to remove the skin

Chop it finely

- Chop the garlic finely

Add salt

- Sprinkle a pinch of salt onto the garlic

Crush the garlic to a paste

- Then crush it into a paste with the side of your knife

It should look like this

- The salt acts as an abrasive surface so you get a smooth paste

Peel and halve the onions

- Peel the onions and chop them in half

Slice horizontally

- Slice the onions horizontally, keeping one hand flat on the top

Slice vertically along the core

- Then slice the onion along the core, but not all the way to the end, so it holds together

Turn the onion 90° and dice finely

- Finally, turn the onion through 90° and dice it finely

Add the oil, onion and garlic

- Put a saucepan on a high heat and add the onion, garlic and olive oil
- Fry the onions and garlic – this should take about 2–3 minutes

Add the mince

- Then add the minced beef to the pan and break it up – this will stop it sticking together

Cook the mince until it's sealed

- Cook the mince until it has sealed (browned all over)
- Keep the mince moving while it's cooking

Add the paprika

- When the beef is sealed we can start to add the other ingredients
- Add the teaspoon of paprika and mix it in

Add the tomato purée

- Add the tomato purée and mix that in before you add anything else

Add the chopped tomatoes

- Then add the chopped, tinned tomatoes and mix them in

Add the other ingredients

- Add the beef stock
- Add the sweet chilli sauce
- Add Worcestershire sauce
- If you don't have sweet chilli sauce, you can use fresh chillies, depending on your taste

Season

- Season well with salt and pepper

Add the kidney beans and simmer

- Drain and rinse the kidney beans
- Add them to the pan as well
- Stir in the kidney beans then turn the heat down
- Simmer for about 20 minutes

Step 2 Making the cheesy corn chips

Put the chips into 4 piles

- When the chilli has about 5 minutes left to cook, you can prepare the cheesy corn chips
- Put the corn chips into 4 separate piles on a baking tray – this makes it easier to separate the chips when you serve them

Sprinkle cheese onto each pile

- Sprinkle each pile with the grated cheese

Melt the cheese

- Put the corn chips under a low grill and melt the cheese gently

Serve

- When the chilli is cooked, ladle it into a bowl and serve it with the corn chips
- When the cheese has melted, serve the corn chips immediately and turn off the grill
- Spoon the sour cream over the chilli to finish
- Add a sprig of parsley for decoration

image taken from video

Sausage Casserole

A one-pot casserole combining Cumberland sausage, fresh vegetables, apples and potatoes – ideal for supper.

Ingredients

- ½ tablespoon olive oil
- 8 medium Cumberland sausages – or 8 home-made ones from the recipe on this DVD
- 1 onion
- 2 small sticks or 1 large stick celery
- 1 medium carrot
- 1 small leek
- 1 large waxy potato
- 1 red-skinned eating apple
- 1 tablespoon plain flour
- ½ tin chopped tomatoes
- 300ml beef or chicken stock
- salt and freshly ground pepper

Optional extras

- 1 bay leaf
- sprig of thyme or pinch of dried chopped thyme

Utensils

- frying pan
- tongs
- kitchen roll
- oven dish
- small chopping knife
- chopping board
- chopping knife
- vegetable peeler
- wooden spoon
- tin foil

A typical serving contains (based on the max. number of people this recipe serves):

Calories	Sugar	Fat	Saturates	Salt
459	9.0g	31g	11g	3.0g
25%	10%	44%	55%	75%

of a child's guideline daily amount

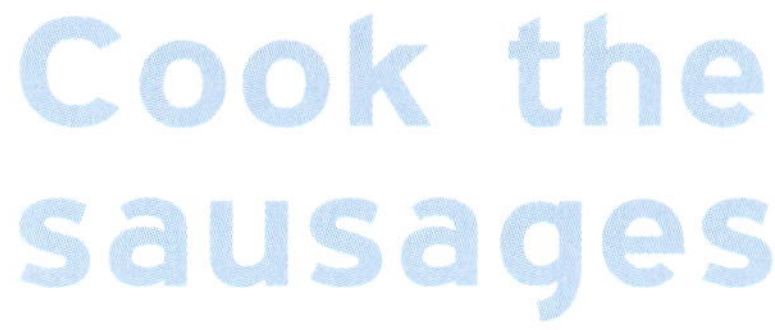

Step 1 Cook the sausages

Put the oil in the frying pan

- Put a frying pan on medium heat and add about ½ tablespoon of olive oil

Add the sausages and cook

- Add the sausages to the pan and fry them until they are lightly browned

Turn occasionally

- Turn them occasionally
- They should take about 10–15 minutes depending on the size

They should be lightly browned

- When the sausages are lightly browned, take them out of the frying pan

Put them in the oven dish

- Drain the sausages slightly on a kitchen towel and put them into the oven dish
- Turn off the heat

Prepare the vegetables

Peel the onion

- First, peel the onion and remove the ends

Cut it into large chunks

- Halve the onion and cut it into large chunks

Slice the celery at an angle

- Wash the celery, then cut off the end
- Slice the celery at an angle and put it in a bowl

Peel the carrot

- Peel the carrot using your vegetable peeler

Cut it in half

- Chop it in half

Cut it into chunks

- Then chop the carrot into chunks and put it in the bowl with the celery

Remove the ends from the leek

- Cut the ends off the leek

Split it in half lengthways

- Split the leek in half lengthways

Wash the leek

- Wash the leek to remove any dirt that might be between the layers

Slice the leek

- Then slice it roughly and add it to the bowl

Peel the potato

- Peel the potato with a vegetable peeler

Chop it into chunks

- Chop the potato into chunks
- Then put it in a bowl of clean water

Quarter the apple

Remove the core

Cut into slices

- Cut the quarters into slices and put them in the bowl of water with the potatoes

Prepare & cook the casserole

Put the vegetables in the frying pan

- Put the celery, onion, leek and carrot into the same pan that was used to cook the sausages, on a medium heat
- Cook the vegetables for 2–3 minutes

Add the flour and mix

- After a couple of minutes, add the tablespoon of flour and mix it in – this will help to thicken the casserole

Add the tomatoes and mix

- Then add the chopped tomatoes and mix them in

Add the stock

Add the bay leaf and dried thyme

- Then add the bay leaf and thyme

Boil, then simmer and season

- Bring the pan to the boil, then simmer for about a minute
- Season with salt and pepper

Add the apple and potato

- Add the apple and potato and mix them in
- Then turn off the heat
- You don't want to cook them too much as they will go too soft and break up

Pour the mix over the sausages

- Pour the vegetable mix over the sausages in the oven dish

Cover with tin foil

- Cover the oven dish with tin foil

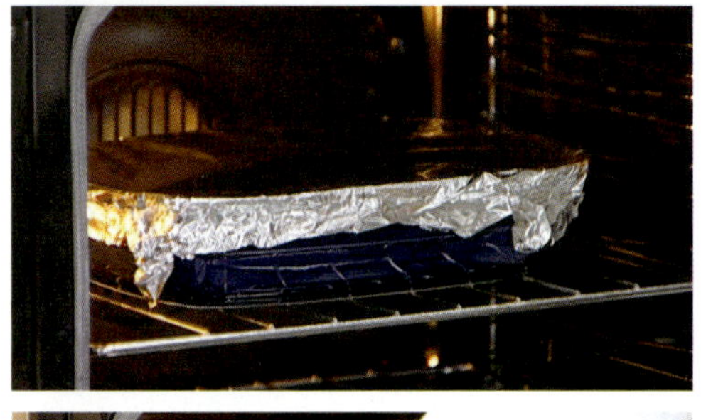

Put casserole in the oven for 1 hour

- Put the casserole in an oven, pre-heated to 180°C (350°F or gas mark 4) for about an hour

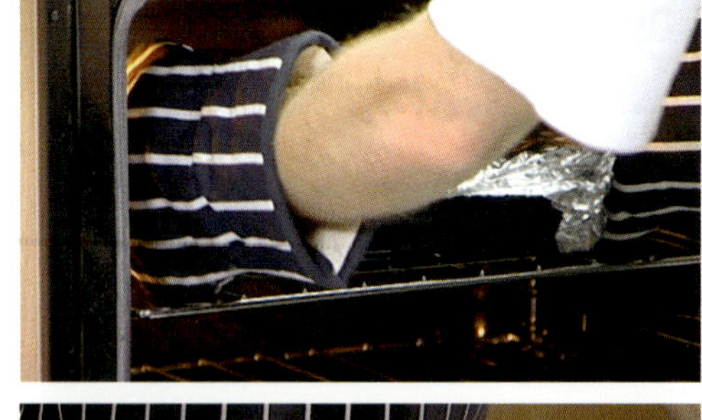

Remove it from the oven

- After an hour, take the casserole out of the oven

Carefully remove the tin foil

- Carefully remove the tin foil and give it a quick stir

Serve

- Serve in a bowl

image taken from video

Aromatic Lamb Burgers

with Crushed Spuds and Raita

A light flavouring of cumin, rosemary and sage provides these 100% lean lamb burgers with their aromatic taste. Served on crushed garlic new potatoes with homemade raita.

RATING  

Ingredients

- 2 stalks of sage or a teaspoon of dried sage
- 2 stalks of rosemary
- 500g good-quality lean minced lamb
- 1 teaspoon cumin
- salt and pepper
- flour for dusting

For the crushed spuds
- 500g new potatoes
- knob of butter
- 1 clove of garlic
- 1 stalk of fresh parsley (plus extra for serving)

For the raita
- 50g cucumber
- 100ml natural yoghurt
- 20g mint sauce

Utensils

- chopping board
- chopping knife
- 2 large mixing bowls
- non-stick frying pan with lid
- spatula
- metal ring
- medium saucepan
- 1 medium mixing bowl
- teaspoon
- cheese grater
- sieve
- tablespoon
- fork

A typical serving contains (based on the max. number of people this recipe serves):

Calories	Sugar	Fat	Saturates	Salt
390	5g	20g	10g	0.5g
22%	6%	28%	50%	12%

of a child's guideline daily amount

Make the burgers

Pick the sage leaves from the stem

- Pick the sage leaves from the stem

Chop the leaves finely

- Chop the sage leaves finely

Pick the rosemary leaves

- Pick the rosemary leaves from the stem

Chop them finely

- Chop the rosemary leaves finely

Put the mince and herbs in a bowl

- Put the lamb mince in a large mixing bowl and add the sage and rosemary

Add the cumin and season

- Add the cumin, salt and black pepper

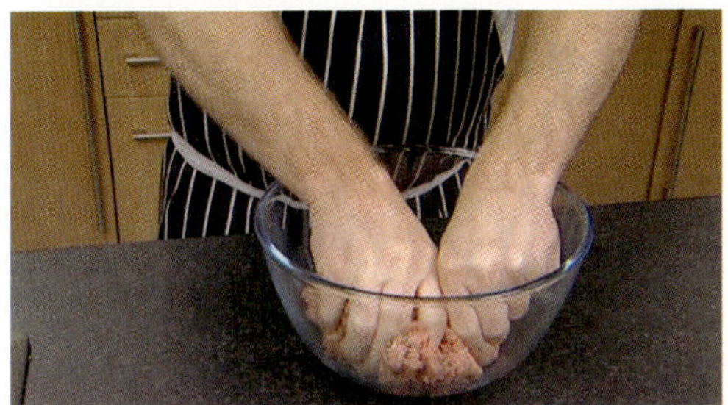

Mix together using your hands

- Mix the lamb and the flavourings together using your hands
- Squeeze it together through your hands

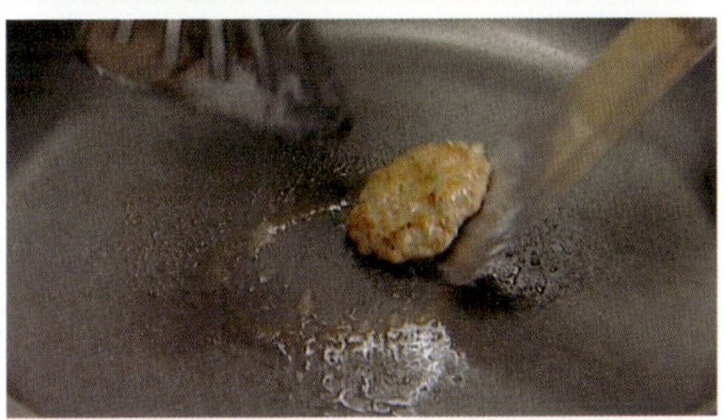

Make a small burger to test

- Put a non-stick frying pan on a medium heat
- If you have a non–stick frying pan, you shouldn't need any oil to cook the lamb in
- Make a small burger shape with a little of the lamb mince and cook it in the frying pan until it has cooked through

Season again if needed

- Taste the small burger to see if the seasoning is right before you make the rest of the burgers
- Add more seasoning if necessary
- Mix the seasoning into the mince with your hands

Flour the table

- Sprinkle the work surface with flour and make the mix into a large ball

Roll into a large sausage shape

- Roll the mix into a large sausage shape

Split in half

- Split the mix in half

Split each half in half again

- Then split each piece in half again

Roll each piece into a ball shape

Press each one into a burger shape

- Make each ball into a burger shape by pressing it into a metal ring
- Put the burgers on a floured plate until you need them
- The burgers will shrink during cooking, so don't worry if they seem big!

Prepare the potatoes

Put a pan of water on to boil

- Make sure you wash the potatoes first if needed
- Put a saucepan of lightly-salted water on to boil

Cut the potatoes

- If the potatoes are large, cut them in half or in three pieces so they will cook a bit quicker

Add the potatoes

- Add the potatoes to the boiling water in the saucepan, then cover and simmer for about 15 minutes, until tender

Step 3 Making the raita

Halve the cucumber

- Before cooking the burgers, make the raita
- Split the cucumber lengthways

Scrape out the seeds

- Scrape out the seeds with a teaspoon and discard them

Grate the cucumber

- Grate all of the remaining cucumber with a cheese grater

Squeeze out the water

- Put the cucumber into a sieve over a bowl and, using a spoon, squeeze all of the water out of it

Into a small bowl

- Put the cucumber into a medium mixing bowl with the yoghurt and mint sauce

Mix thoroughly

- Mix it together thoroughly

Season with salt and mix

- Add a pinch of salt and mix
- That's it!

Cook the burgers

Put the burgers in the frying pan

- Put the burgers in the frying pan on a medium heat

Turn them

- After a few minutes, check the burgers are brown and turn them over
- Cook for a few more minutes

Continue to cook them

- When the burgers have browned on both sides, turn the heat down to low to cook them all the way through
- This should take about 8–10 minutes
- Turn the burgers every so often so they don't burn

Prepare the garlic and parsley

- Now prepare the garlic and parsley that you will use to flavour the potatoes
- Pick the parsley leaves from the stem

Chop them finely

- Chop the parsley leaves finely

Peel the garlic

- Crush the garlic under your knife to remove the skin

Chop it finely

- Chop the garlic finely

Test the potatoes

- Check the potatoes are soft with a knife – if they are, they're cooked
- Turn off the heat

Put them in a bowl

- Drain the potatoes and put them in a bowl
- Add the knob of butter

Add garlic and parsley, then season

- Then add the garlic and parsley
- Season with salt and pepper

Crush with a fork

- Using a fork, crush the potatoes, but don't mash them too finely

Test the burgers are cooked

- To check if the burgers are cooked, cut into one with a knife – if the juices run clear they are ready
- Turn off the heat

Serve

- Serve the burger on a bed of potatoes and top with the raita

image taken from video

Hot Pot

The classic of all classics, using lean neck fillet of lamb and bundles of fresh vegetables, topped with thinly sliced potatoes and oven-baked. A great family dish!

SERVES 4 PEOPLE

Ingredients

- 450g neck fillet or diced lamb
- salt and pepper
- 1 leek
- 2 carrots
- 2 celery sticks
- 1 onion
- 1 clove of garlic
- 2 large sprigs fresh rosemary
- fresh chopped parsley
- a little olive oil
- 700ml chicken stock
- 4 large potatoes
- 50g butter (melted)

Utensils

- small chopping knife
- chopping knife
- chopping board
- frying pan
- oven dish
- vegetable peeler
- large mixing bowl
- wooden spoon
- pastry brush

A typical serving contains (based on the max. number of people this recipe serves):

Calories	Sugar	Fat	Saturates	Salt
512	10g	22g	7.0g	0.6g
28%	10%	31%	35%	15%

of a child's guideline daily amount

Prepare & pre-cook the lamb

Remove the sinew and fat

- Remove the sinew and fat from the lamb neck fillet

Dice the lamb

- Cut the lamb into cubes, each 1–2cm in size

Put the diced lamb in the frying pan

- Put the lamb in a dry frying pan on a high heat

Seal the lamb

- Fry the lamb for a few minutes until it is sealed (browned all over)

Season with salt and pepper

- Season the lamb lightly with salt and pepper

Put the lamb into the oven dish

- Put the lamb into a large oven dish

Prepare & pre-cook the vegetables

Remove the ends of the leek

- Remove the ends of the leek and discard

Split the leek lengthways

- Split the leek along its length

Wash the leek

- Wash the leek in a bowl of water or under the tap

Slice the leek

- Slice the leek finely and put it to one side in a bowl

Peel the carrots

- Peel the carrots with a vegetable peeler, removing the ends

Split in half lengthways

- Split the carrot lengthways, then split each half in half again

Chop into small chunks

- Chop it into small chunks and put it in the bowl with the leeks

Remove the leaves from the celery

- Remove the leaves from the celery

Slice the celery

- Slice the celery finely and add it to the bowl

Peel the onion

- Peel the onion, then halve it and remove the ends

Slice horizontally

- Slice the onion horizontally with your hand flat on the top

Chop along the core

- Then slice along the core, but not all the way to the end

Turn through 90° and chop again

- Turn the onion then dice it finely and add it to the bowl

Peel the garlic

- Peel the garlic by crushing it with your knife and then pulling off the skin

Chop it finely

- Chop the garlic finely
- Put the chopped garlic in the bowl

Pick the rosemary leaves

- Pick the rosemary leaves from the stem

Chop them finely

- Chop the rosemary leaves finely

Pick the parsley leaves

- Pick the parsley leaves from the stem

Chop them finely

- Chop them as well

Add the oil and vegetables to pan

- Put a frying pan on a medium heat and add a little olive oil
- Add all of the vegetables and fry for a couple of minutes

Add the rosemary and parsley

- Add the chopped rosemary and parsley and mix them in

Season

- Season with salt and pepper

Add the vegetables to the oven dish

- When the vegetables have fried for 2–3 minutes, add them to the oven dish with the lamb and mix them together
- Turn off the heat

Add the stock

- Pour the stock over the top so that it just covers the lamb and vegetables

Prepare the potatoes & cook

Peel the potatoes

- First peel the potatoes with a vegetable peeler and put them in a bowl of cold water

Remove a slice

- Take a potato and remove a slice from the side – this will enable you to lay it flat and make it easier to slice

Thinly slice the potatoes

- Lay the potatoes flat and slice them thinly (you can also use a slicer for this to get them very thin)

Lay the slices on top

- Lay the slices of potato onto the top of the hot pot, overlapping them slightly
- Gently press the potatoes down into the hot pot

Melt the butter in the microwave

- Melt the 50g butter in the microwave – it should only take about 30 seconds

Brush the potatoes with the butter

- Using a pastry brush, coat the top of the potatoes with the melted butter

Put the dish in the oven

- Put the dish in an oven, pre-heated to 160°C (325°F or gas mark 3) for 1 hour 15 minutes

Remove after 1 hour 15 minutes

- Remove the dish from the oven after it has cooked – the potatoes should have turned a golden brown on the top
- Turn off the oven

Serve

- Serve and enjoy!

image taken from video

Chicken Burgers

A healthy chicken burger, lightly flavoured with sage and onion, served on a toasted sesame bun with reduced-fat mayo and iceberg lettuce.

PREP TIME **25** MINUTES

COOK TIME **15** MINUTES

SERVES **4** PEOPLE

RATING  

Ingredients

- 100g fresh breadcrumbs
- 1 onion
- ½ tablespoon olive oil
- 1 teaspoon of dried sage
- 4 chicken thighs
- salt and pepper
- plain flour (for dusting)
- 1 beef tomato or 2 normal tomatoes
- ¼ of a medium iceberg lettuce
- 4 sesame buns
- 50g light/low-fat mayonnaise

Utensils

- bread knife
- chopping board
- food processor
- medium mixing bowl
- small chopping knife
- frying pan with lid
- wooden spoon
- palette knife
- knife

A typical serving contains (based on the max. number of people this recipe serves):

Calories	Sugar	Fat	Saturates	Salt
420	5.0g	11g	2.0g	1.9g
23%	6%	15%	10%	47%

of a child's guideline daily amount

Make the burger mix

Remove crusts from the bread

- Cut the crusts off the bread and chop it into chunks

Put the bread in a food processor

- Put the bread in a food processor and blend for about a minute until it has turned into breadcrumbs

Put in a bowl and keep to one side

- Put the breadcrumbs in a bowl and keep them to one side until you need them

Peel and halve the onion

- Peel the onion and chop it in half

Slice horizontally

- Lay the ½ onion on the flat and slice it horizontally with your hand flat on the top

Dice

- Slice the onion along the centre
- Then turn it through 90° and dice it finely
- Repeat with the other half of the onion

Fry the onions

- Put the chopped onion in a frying pan on a medium heat with ½ tablespoon of olive oil
- Fry lightly

Add the dried sage

- Once the onions have cooked for 2–3 minutes, add the teaspoon of dried sage
- Then mix and turn off the heat
- Allow to cool

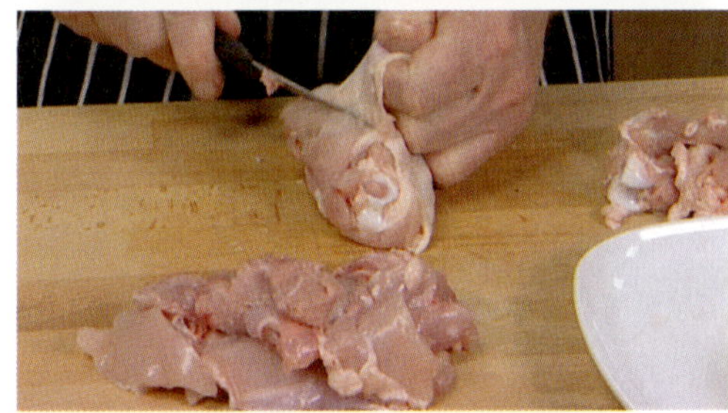

Prepare the chicken

- Remove the skin from the chicken thighs

Cut the meat away from the bone

- Carefully cut the meat away from the bones

Remove any sinew and fat

- Remove any excess sinew and fat from the chicken

Cut the chicken into chunks

- Cut the meat into small chunks

Put the chicken in the Processor

- Put the chicken in the food processor

Pulse – you don't want it too fine

- Just pulse the chicken in the food processor – you don't want to chop it too finely or it will become too liquid
- You want a mince-like texture

Add the fried onions and sage

- Then add the fried onions and sage

Add the breadcrumbs and season

- Add the breadcrumbs
- Season with salt and pepper

Pulse the mix together

- Pulse the mix again to mix the ingredients together

Make a small burger to test

- Make a small burger with a little of the chicken mix

Cook in the frying pan and taste

- Put a frying pan on a high heat and cook the chicken burger mix in a little olive oil
- When the chicken is cooked, taste it to check you've got the seasoning right
- You can season the mix again now, if needed
- Take the pan off the heat

Make the burgers

Flour a table and turn out the mix

- Flour the work surface and turn out the mix

Roll into a large sausage shape

- Roll the chicken mix in the flour and into a large sausage shape

Split in half

- Split the mix in half

Split each half in half again

- Then split each half in half again

Roll into balls

- Roll the mix into 4 balls

Press down into a metal ring

- Then press each ball into a metal ring to make it burger shaped

Neaten with a palette knife

- Neaten the burgers with a palette knife, if needed
- Put them on a floured plate until you cook them

Cook & serve

Prepare the tomatoes

- Remove the stalk from the tomatoes and slice

Remove the core from the lettuce

- Remove the core from the iceberg lettuce

Shred the lettuce

- Then slice finely or shred the lettuce

Add oil and burgers to the pan

- Put the frying pan back on the high heat with the ½ tablespoon of oil
- Add the burgers to the pan and cook them for about 5 minutes

Turn

- After about 5 minutes, turn the burgers in the frying pan when they have browned on one side
- Keep turning the burgers to brown them evenly and cook them through

Test the burgers are cooked

- To check the burgers are cooked, cut one open with a knife and make sure it's not pink in the middle. If it's white all the way through, its ready – if not cook for longer
- Turn off the heat and leave the burgers in the pan to keep them warm

Toast the buns

- Cut the sesame buns in half and put them on the grill tray

Toast under grill

- Toast them under the grill until they are lightly browned

Build the burgers

- Put a dollop of mayonnaise onto the bottom half of each bun

Put a burger on each one

- Put the burger onto the mayo

Add tomato

- Put a slice of tomato on top of each burger

Add lettuce

- Add the shredded lettuce

Top and serve

- Finally, top the burgers and serve
- Here we have used sandwich sticks to hold the burgers together, which are safer than cocktail sticks

Treats

image taken from video

Chocolate Brownies

An American classic! Lightly spiced with cloves, ginger and cinnamon. Chopped walnuts provide the crunch. A great snack for children and adults alike!

PREP TIME **30** MINUTES | COOK TIME **30** MINUTES | MAKES **10+** BARS

RATING   

Ingredients

- 160g butter (soft)
- 100g flour
- 1 teaspoon baking powder
- 30g cocoa powder
- pinch of cinnamon powder
- pinch of ground ginger
- pinch of salt
- ½ a teaspoon of ground cloves
- 2 ½ large eggs (3 eggs)
- 1 egg yolk
- 64g walnuts
- 160g caster sugar
- 2ml vanilla essence

For the topping/glaze

- 150g dark baker's chocolate (cooking chocolate/cake covering)
- 25g butter

Utensils

- large baking tin or cake tin
- baking paper
- scissors
- 2 large mixing bowls
- sieve
- 2 medium mixing bowls
- fork
- 2 small mixing bowls
- chopping knife
- chopping board
- silicone spatula
- wire rack
- saucepan
- palette knife
- serrated knife

A typical serving contains (based on the max. number of people this recipe serves):

Calories	Sugar	Fat	Saturates	Salt
302	16g	21g	10g	0.6g
17%	19%	30%	50%	15%

of a child's guideline daily amount

Prepare & make the mix

Measure the baking paper and cut

- Measure the baking paper so it's big enough to cover the base and the sides of the tin

Trim away any excess

- Cut the paper to size, trimming away any excess

Cut in from the corners

- Cut in diagonally from the corners of the paper towards the centre – this is so you can fold the paper and cover the sides of the tin

Butter the cake tin

- Rub butter all over the inside of the cake tin

Push the baking paper into the tin

- Line the baking tin with baking paper, making sure to press it into all the corners
- Add a little more butter if the paper doesn't stick properly

Sieve

- Sieve the flour, baking powder, cocoa powder, cinnamon, ginger, salt and ground cloves together into a large mixing bowl

Crack the egg and beat

- Crack 1 egg into a small bowl and beat it with a fork

Split the egg in half

- Split the egg in half (we will only use half of this egg)

Crack the other 2 eggs and beat

- Crack the 2 eggs into another mixing bowl and beat them

Add ½ the first egg

- Add ½ of the first egg, so that you have 2½ beaten eggs in the same bowl

Separate the yolk from the last egg

- Separate the yolk from the final egg

Add the yolk to the beaten eggs

- Add the yolk to the bowl as well

Beat in the yolk

- Beat all the eggs together with a fork

Chop the walnuts

- Chop the walnuts and put them to one side for later

Put the sugar and butter in a bowl

- Put the 160g of butter and the 160g caster sugar in a large mixing bowl

Mix the butter into the sugar

- Start to mix the butter and sugar together using your hands

When combined, beat together

- When the butter and sugar are combined, begin to beat them together more vigorously
- It's easier to use your hands for this, but make sure you wash them first!

It should go light, fluffy and creamy

- After a while, the mix should turn light and fluffy

Add the egg mix, a little at a time

- When the mix is light and fluffy, slowly begin to add the egg
- Add only a little at a time

Mix each drop of egg in thoroughly

- Make sure you mix the egg in thoroughly each time so that it is completely combined
- There is a lot of work involved in this!!

Continue to add the egg

- Continue to add the egg in this way until it is all gone

If it splits, add some flour mix

- If the mix splits and goes grainy while you are adding the egg (it should be smooth), add about a tablespoon of the sieved flour mixture

Mix in the flour

- Mix the flour in thoroughly – this will help combine it again and make it smooth

Add the remainder of the flour mix

- When you have used all of the egg mix, add the rest of the flour mix

Add a few drops of vanilla essence

- Add a few drops of vanilla essence

Add the chopped walnuts

- Then add the chopped walnuts

Fold it together

- Fold the mix together with a silicone spatula

It should look like this

- The mix should have a smooth consistency

Cook the brownies

Spoon the mix into the tin

- Spoon the brownie mix into your lined tin
- Use the silicone spatula to spread it out and press it into all of the corners
- Make sure it is only about 2cm deep (you may need to use more than one tin if you don't have a large one)

Put it in the oven

- Put the baking tin in the oven, pre-heated to 190°C (375°F or gas mark 5) for 20 minutes

Remove it after 20 minutes

- After 20 minutes, remove the brownie from the oven

Test it's cooked

- Check the brownie is cooked by pressing the top down slightly – it should spring back to shape slightly, but not all the way
- Leave the brownie to cool for 10 minutes

Turn it out onto the wire rack

- After 10 minutes, turn the brownie out of the tin onto a wire rack
- Use oven gloves if the tin is still hot
- First put the rack on top of the tin

Carefully turn both over together

- Then carefully turn both over together like this

Lift off the tin

- Carefully lift off the tin

Remove the baking paper and cool

- Remove the baking paper and leave the brownie to cool completely to room temperature before glazing and cutting

Step 3 Glazing

Melt the chocolate and butter

- While the brownie is cooling, put a mixing bowl on a pan of simmering water so that the water isn't touching the bottom of the bowl (this is called a bain marie)
- Break the chocolate into small pieces and put it in the mixing bowl with the butter

Stir until completely melted

- Be careful not to get any water in the bowl as it will turn the chocolate grainy and ruin it
- Stir the chocolate and butter in the bowl occasionally until completely melted
- The butter keeps the chocolate softer for when you cut the brownies

Pour on the glaze

- Pour the glaze onto the top of the now cool brownie

Spread it out

- Spread the glaze to all the edges using a palette knife

Neaten the edges

- Spread the knife along the sides of the brownie to stop any drips and neaten it

Make a pattern on the top

- Make a pattern on top with your knife
- Leave the chocolate glaze to set

Cut & serve

Cut into bars

- When the chocolate is set you can cut the brownie into bars
- Cut it in half, and then into bars – that's it!

Serve

- Serve and enjoy!

Image taken from video

Apple Pie

Classic home-made pie with piquant bramley apples and cinnamon. Great served hot or cold with cream, ice cream or custard.

PREP TIME **1** HOUR

COOK TIME **45** MINUTES

MAKES **8** PORTIONS

RATING   

Ingredients

*For the sweet pastry**
- 250g soft flour (plus more for rolling out)
- 70g caster sugar
- pinch of salt
- 125g butter or cooking margerine
- 1 small egg
- 25ml water

**You can buy ready-made sweet pastry from the supermarket*

For the apple filling
- 3 bramley apples (cooking)
- 25ml water
- 10g caster sugar
- ½ teaspoon cinnamon (optional)

- granulated sugar, to sprinkle
- butter, to grease
- water, to brush the pie
- icing sugar, to dust

Utensils

- large mixing bowl
- fork
- cling film
- vegetable peeler
- small knife
- chopping board
- medium saucepan
- wooden spoon
- round cake tin
- baking paper
- kitchen scissors
- rolling pin
- pastry brush
- oven gloves
- plate

A typical serving contains (based on the max. number of people this recipe serves):

Calories	Sugar	Fat	Saturates	Salt
390	21g	18g	11g	0.5g
22%	25%	26%	55%	12%

of a child's guideline daily amount

Put the dry ingredients in a bowl

- Put the flour, sugar, salt and butter in a large mixing bowl

Rub the butter in

- Rub the butter into the other ingredients using your fingertips

It should resemble breadcrumbs

- Keep rubbing until it resembles fine breadcrumbs

Make it finer

- After a while, rub the mix through your hands to make it finer again

Make a well in the centre

- Make a well in the centre of the mix and crack the egg into it

Beat the egg

- Beat the egg in the centre of the bowl with a fork

Add the water and continue to beat

- Then add the water and continue to beat

Combine the mix

- When it's thoroughly beaten, begin to combine the egg and water with the butter and flour mix using your hand

Turn it out

- Turn the pastry dough out onto the work surface
- Gather all the bits together

It should begin to form into a ball

- Knead the pastry, keeping it dusted with flour
- If it sticks to your hands, rub a little flour in them to remove it

It should go smooth

- Knead the pastry until it goes smooth and silky – this should take about 2–3 minutes

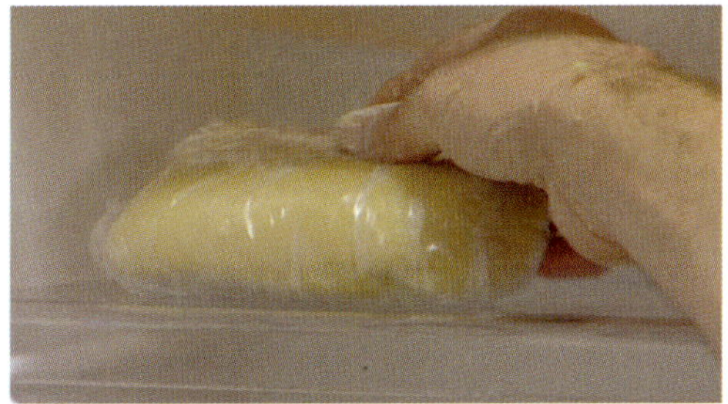

Put it in the fridge

- Wrap the ball of pastry in cling film and put it in the fridge to firm it up
- The dough will last in the fridge for about a week if it is covered

Prepare & cook the apples

Peel the apples

- Peel the apples with a vegetable peeler

Quarter the apples

- Cut the apples into quarters

Remove the core

- Cut out the core from each piece

Chop it into chunks

- Chop the apples into chunks

Put the apples in a saucepan

- Put the apples in a medium saucepan with 25ml of water
- Add the caster sugar

Add the cinnamon and cook

- Add the cinnamon and turn the heat to medium

Give them a stir and put the lid on

- Cook the apples for 5–6 minutes, stirring occasionally

They will have softened

- After 5–6 minutes, the apples will go soft
- Take them off the heat and turn it off

Step 3 Make the pie

Measure the baking paper

- Cut a square of baking paper larger than the round cake tin

Cut off any excess

- Cut off any excess paper

Fold it in half 4 times

- Fold the paper in half 4 times (so the paper is triangular in shape)

Measure the radius of the tin

- Measure the paper to cover the radius of the tin, and add a little more to allow for the sides

Cut to size

- Cut the paper to fit the tin – a curved cut

Cut strips in the end

- Cut several strips in from the end – cut about the depth of the tin

Butter the tin

- Rub the baking tin with butter

Press the baking paper into the tin

- Press the baking paper into the tin, making sure it goes into all the corners

Break off two-thirds of the pastry

- Take the pastry out of the fridge
- Break off about two-thirds of the pastry and knead it slightly with your hands

Roll it out

- Flour the work surface and roll out the pastry into a circle until it is bigger than the baking tin and about ½cm thick (you need enough to cover the sides as well as the base)

It should be bigger than the tin

- Make sure you roll the pastry out so it is big enough to cover the base and the sides of the tin

Roll it onto the rolling pin

- Roll the pastry up onto your rolling pin

Then unroll it onto the tin

- Carefully unroll it onto the tin

Push it into the edges

- Carefully press the pastry down into all of the edges of the tin, leaving an overhang at the top

Add the apples

- Put the apple filling in the pastry case and flatten it down slightly

Roll out the remaining pastry

- Roll out the remaining pastry into a circle – again it should be about ½cm thick and slightly larger than the tin

Brush the rim with water

- Brush the rim of the pie with a little water

Roll the top on and seal

- Roll the pastry up onto your rolling pin and unroll it over the top of the pie
- Press the top and bottom layers of the pastry together around the edge

Trim

- Trim the excess pastry away from the edges

Pinch the edges together

- Then pinch the pastry together around the rim all the way around

Cut a hole in the top

- Cut a small hole in the top of the pie to let the steam out

Finish the pie

- Brush the top of the pie with water
- Sprinkle with granulated sugar

Step 4 Cook & serve

Put it in the oven

- Put the pie in the oven at 180°C (350°F or gas mark 4) for 30–40 minutes

Take it out of the oven

- The pastry should be light brown on the top when it's cooked
- Take the pie out of the oven and leave it to cool completely in the tin for at least 20 minutes

When it's cool, put a plate on top

- To take the pie out of the tin, when its cool, put a plate on top

Turn over and remove the tin

- Turn the plate and tin over together
- Carefully lift off the tin

Remove the baking paper

- Remove the baking paper from the base of the pie

Turn it upright

- Then put another plate on top of the pie and turn it back over so the pie is the right way up for serving

Cut a slice

- Cut a slice of the pie and put it on a plate

Serve

- Dust with icing sugar to serve
- This is also great served with cream!

image taken from video

Caramelised Rice Pudding

Hot, creamy rice pudding with real vanilla seeds, topped with caramelised muscavado sugar. A good tip is not to put the caster sugar in the rice pudding mix until right at the end, as the sugar is what can cause the pudding to burn on the bottom!

PREP TIME **5** MINUTES

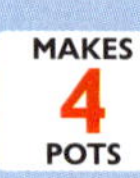

Ingredients

- 1 vanilla pod
- 1 litre semi-skimmed milk
- 130ml single cream
- 110g pudding rice
- pinch of grated nutmeg
- 50g butter
- 25g caster sugar
- dark brown Muscavado sugar (to caramelise the tops)

Utensils

- small chopping knife
- chopping board
- medium saucepan
- wooden spoon
- teaspoon
- 4 ramekins or small pots, to serve
- baking tray
- oven gloves

A typical serving contains (based on the max. number of people this recipe serves):

Calories	Sugar	Fat	Saturates	Salt
416	23g	22g	10g	0.5g
23%	27%	31%	50%	12%

of a child's guideline daily amount

Make the pudding

Split the vanilla pod

- Split the vanilla pod along its length

Scrape out the seeds

- Scrape the seeds out of each half of the pod

Boil the milk and cream

- Put the milk and cream in a medium saucepan on a medium heat and bring them to the boil

Add the pod and the seeds

- Then put the whole vanilla pod (skin and seeds) in the pan

When boiling, add the rice

- As soon as the pan comes to the boil, add the rice
- Turn the heat right down and simmer

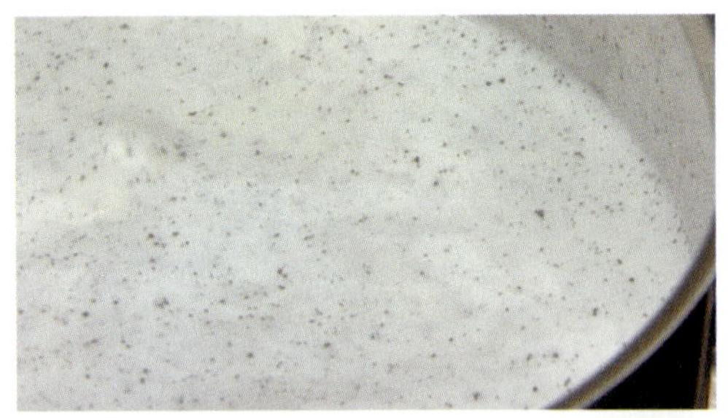

Simmer for 30 minutes

- Keep stirring the mix so it doesn't stick to the bottom
- Simmer until it's cooked – this should take around 30 minutes

It should have thickened

- After 30 or 40 minutes the rice should be soft and cooked and the mix should have thickened

Add the nutmeg and butter

- Add the pinch of nutmeg and the butter

Add the caster sugar and mix

- Add the caster sugar and mix it in until it has melted

Remove the vanilla pod skin

- Carefully take out the vanilla pod skin

It should be thick and creamy

- The pudding should be thick and creamy

Caramelise & serve

Put the pudding in pots

- Spoon the rice pudding into your small serving pots
- This rice pudding is great served like this but you can also caramelise the top

Cover the tops with brown sugar

- Sprinkle the rice puddings with muscavado sugar, completely covering them

Put them under the grill

- Then melt the sugar by putting the pots on a baking tray and under a hot grill for 1–2 minutes

The sugar should bubble

- When the sugar turns dark and bubbles, it's ready!
- Remove the pots and turn off the oven
- Leave it to cool and harden

Serve

- A great winter warmer!

image taken from video

Little Chocolate Mousse Pots

Rich dark chocolate pots topped with fluffy, whipped cream and a chocolate decoration. Make sure you use fresh, free-range eggs.

PREP TIME **20** MINUTES

COOK TIME **20** MINUTES

MAKES **4–8** POTS

RATING

Ingredients

- 200g milk or dark chocolate
- 150ml single cream
- 4 eggs (4 yolks and 3 whites)
- 50g caster sugar
- 100ml whipping cream, for decoration
- 1 teaspoon icing sugar
- icing sugar, to dust

Utensils

- medium saucepan
- large mixing bowl
- wooden spoon
- small plate
- cling film
- 3 medium or small mixing bowls
- whisk
- electric hand-held whisk
- large jug
- glasses or pots, to serve
- tablespoon
- silicone spoon/spatula

A typical serving contains (based on the max. number of people this recipe serves):

Calories	Sugar	Fat	Saturates	Salt
547	28g	36g	20g	0.2g
30%	33%	51%	100%	5%

of a child's guideline daily amount

WARNING!

This recipe uses raw egg – make sure you use fresh, free-range or pasteurised eggs. It is not suitable for babies or pregnant women.

Step 1 Make the mix

Melt the chocolate in a 'bain marie'

- Melt the chocolate in a 'bain marie' over a pan of simmering water
- Don't let the water touch the bottom of the bowl as it will get too hot and burn the chocolate!

Wrap a plate in cling film

- When the chocolate has completely melted wrap a plate in cling film

Drizzle the chocolate

- Drizzle a little of the chocolate from a wooden spoon onto the cling film to make a nice pattern

Put it in the fridge

- Put the plate in the fridge until the chocolate is set – this should take at least 10 minutes

Separate the 3 egg yolks and whites

- Separate the 3 egg yolks and whites

Separate the yolk from the last egg

- Separate the yolk from the last egg, but discard the white

Whisk the 3 egg whites

- Next, in a clean bowl whip the 3 egg whites until you can make soft peaks in them

Add the caster sugar and whisk

- Then add the caster sugar and whisk it in

Soft peaks

- There should be soft peaks in the egg whites

Add the cream to the chocolate

- Add the cream (150ml) to the chocolate and mix it in

Add the 4 yolks to the mix

- Add the 4 egg yolks to the chocolate mix

Whisk

- Whisk the yolks in

Whisk until it thickens

- Whisk until the mix thickens, just to cook the eggs – this should take 7–8 minutes
- Then turn off the heat and remove the bowl from the saucepan

Add the chocolate mix

- Pour the chocolate mix into the egg whites

Fold in gently

- Fold the mix together gently

Pour it into a jug

- When completely combined, pour the mix into a large jug – this will make it easier to pour it into the serving glasses or pots

Pour it into glasses or pots

- Pour the mousse mix into the glasses or pots you will serve it in

Put them in the fridge

- Put the glasses in the fridge until the mousse has set (at least an hour – preferably overnight) before you progress to Step 2

Step 2 Serve

Add some icing sugar to the cream

- When you are ready to serve the chocolate pots, add a teaspoon of icing sugar to the whipping cream

Whisk until light and fluffy

- Whip the cream (100ml) in a large mixing bowl, increasing the speed as you go

It should look like this

- It should be light and fluffy

Scoop out the cream

- Using a hot, wet spoon, scoop out a spoonful of cream to go on the top of each mousse pot

It should look like this

- Try and make nice, neat curls

Spoon the cream onto the pots

- Put a spoonful of cream on top of each pot

Add the chocolate decoration

- Remove the chocolate decoration from the fridge
- Carefully remove the chocolate from the plate using a spatula

Break it up and put it on top

- Break it roughly into 4 and put it on top of the cream in each pot

Serve

- To finish, dust the desserts with icing sugar

image taken from video

Orange & Marmalade Bread & Butter Pudding

A traditional favourite with fresh vanilla seeds, finished with orange marmalade.

PREP TIME 15 MINUTES

COOK TIME 50 MINUTES

SERVES 4–8 PEOPLE

RATING 

Ingredients

- 12 slices medium or 8 slices thick white bread
- 100g butter (softened)
- 2 whole eggs
- 4 egg yolks
- 175g caster sugar
- 1 vanilla pod or a few drops of vanilla essence
- 1 large orange (zest)
- 100ml double cream
- 500ml semi-skimmed milk
- 25g sultanas
- 100g orange marmalade
- double cream (to serve)

Utensils

- large oven dish
- spreading knife
- chopping board
- bread knife
- 1 large mixing bowl
- 1 medium mixing bowl
- small chopping knife
- cheese grater
- medium saucepan
- sieve
- whisk
- ladle
- potato masher
- small saucepan
- wooden spoon
- pastry brush

A typical serving contains (based on the max. number of people this recipe serves):

Calories	Sugar	Fat	Saturates	Salt
615	49g	31g	17g	1.2g
34%	58%	44%	85%	30%

of a child's guideline daily amount

Make the pudding

Lightly butter a large oven dish

Butter the bread

Remove the crusts

Cut it into triangles

- Cut the bread into triangles, then put them to one side for later

Crack 2 whole eggs into a bowl

- Crack the 2 whole eggs into a large mixing bowl

Separate the yolks and add to bowl

- Take the 4 remaining eggs
- Seperate the yolks from the egg whites and add the yolks to the bowl
- Discard the egg whites

Add the caster sugar and mix

- Add the caster sugar
- Whisk the mix together

Keep whisking until combined

- Keep whisking the mix until it combines together to make a smooth mixture like this

Split the vanilla pod

- Use a knife to split the vanilla pod in two lengthways

Scrape out the seeds

- Scraping out the seeds will help the flavouring

Grate the orange

- Grate the orange to remove the orange zest
- We don't want any of the white pith, which is under the orange skin

Add the double cream and milk

- Pour the double cream and the milk into a saucepan

Add the vanilla pod and the seeds

Boil, then turn off the heat

- Bring the mix to the boil on a medium heat
- When it boils turn off the heat

Sieve into the egg mixtue

- Pour the cream and milk mix through a sieve into the beaten eggs

Whisk

- Whisk the mixture together until it becomes smooth

Add the orange zest and whisk

- Add the grated orange zest to the bowl
- Whisk together thoroughly

Layer the bread in the oven dish

- Place a layer of the bread in the bottom of the bowl

Sprinkle over all of the sultanas

- Sprinkle the sultanas on top

Cover with the remaining bread

- Make sure you cover all of the sultanas with bread – otherwise they will burn in the oven

Ladle the custard over the top

- Ladle all of the custard evenly over the bread making sure all of the bread is covered

Press the bread into the custard

- Press the bread down using a potato masher to help it absorb as much custard as possible

Leave to absorb for 30 minutes

- Leave the pudding for 30 minutes to allow it to absorb the custard

Cook & serve

Into the oven

- Put the pudding in the oven at 170°c (325°F or gas mark 3) for 30–40 minutes

Melt the marmalade

- Just before the pudding is ready, begin to melt the marmalade on a low heat

Stir until completely melted

- Stir the marmalade until it's completely melted

Take the pudding out of the oven

- The pudding is ready when it is lightly browned on the top and the custard has set
- Turn off the oven
- Brush melted marmalade over the top using a pastry brush

Serve

- Serve and enjoy!

image taken from video

Honey & Pumpkin Seed Oaty Bars

A fruit-and-nut-style flapjack packed with oats. A great alternative snack that won't last long in the biscuit tin!

PREP TIME **10** MINUTES | COOK TIME **30** MINUTES | MAKES **12** BARS

RATING    

Ingredients

- 80g butter
- 80g soft dark brown sugar
- pinch of salt
- 60g golden syrup
- 40g honey
- 40g dried apple (chopped)
- 140g porridge oats
- 50g sunflower seeds
- 50g pumpkin seeds
- 40g desiccated coconut

Utensils

- medium saucepan
- wooden spoon
- small chopping knife
- chopping board
- 18cm-square cake tin
- baking paper
- kitchen scissors
- large mixing bowl
- silicone spatula/spoon
- potato masher
- large chopping knife

A typical serving contains (based on the max. number of people this recipe serves):

Calories	Sugar	Fat	Saturates	Salt
216	15g	12g	6.0g	0.2g
12%	18%	17%	30%	5%

of a child's guideline daily amount

Make the mix

Put the butter in a saucepan

- Melt 40g of the butter on a medium heat in a medium saucepan

Add the brown sugar and some salt

- Add the brown sugar
- Add a pinch of salt
- Mix together thoroughly

Add the golden syrup and honey

- When the butter has melted, add the golden syrup and the honey

Stir to help it melt

- Give the mixture a quick stir to ensure it's all melting
- When it's melted, turn off the heat

Chop the dried apple

- Chop the dried apple into small pieces

Line the cake tin

- Line a 10cm-square cake tin by laying the tin on the baking paper
- Cut the paper larger than the tin – large enough to cover the bottom and the sides

Cut off any excess

- Cut off any excess paper

Cut in from the corners

- Cut in from the corners towards the centre

Rub butter inside the tin

- Rub butter all over the inside of the tin (this helps the paper stick to the tin)

Push the paper down into the tin

- Press the baking paper down into the tin, making sure it goes into all the corners
- Add a little more butter if the paper doesn't stick properly

Put the oats and seeds in a bowl

- Put the oats and sunflower seeds in the large mixing bowl

Add the pumpkin seeds

- Add the pumpkin seeds to the bowl

Add the desiccated coconut

- Add the desiccated coconut

Add the chopped apple

- Add the chopped apple as well

Mix thoroughly

- Mix the dry ingredients together thoroughly

Add the melted mix

- Add the melted mix to the bowl

Mix together well

- Mix well until all of the dry ingredients are coated with the honey and syrup mix

Cook & serve

Put the mix into the lined cake tin

- Spoon the mixture into the tin

Push it to the sides with a spatula

- Spread it to the edges and into the corners with the spatula

Press it down flat

- Press the mixture down into the tin with a potato masher to level the top

Put it in the oven

- Bake at 180°C (350°F or gas mark 4) for 18–20 minutes

Remove when cooked

- After 20 minutes, it should be cooked and lightly browned on the top
- Turn off the oven
- Leave it to cool for at least 1 hour (this will allow it to firm up so it's not too gooey when you cut and serve it)

When cool, lift it out of the cake tin

- When it is cool, carefully lift it out of the tin by the baking paper

Remove the baking paper

- Put it on a chopping board and carefully remove the baking paper

Cut in half one way

- Cut it in half one way

Then the other

- Then the other

Then into bars

- Finally, cut it into bars

Serve

image taken from video

Super Fruit Trifles

A colourful, fruity version of the traditional dessert with strawberries, blueberries and raspberries. Topped with freshly-whipped cream.

PREP TIME **20** MINUTES | COOK TIME **10** MINUTES | MAKES **6–8** TRIFLES | RATING  

Ingredients

- 12 sponge fingers
- 100g strawberries
- 50g blueberries
- 50g raspberries
- 570ml or 1 pint of jelly (1 x 135g pack of jelly squares plus water to make it up to 1 pint)
- icing sugar, (to dust and for sweetening the cream)
- 250ml whipping cream

For the custard

- 35g caster sugar
- 50g custard powder
- 1 pint semi-skimmed milk

Utensils

- glasses, to serve
- chopping board
- small chopping knife
- measuring jug
- medium mixing bowl
- fork
- whisk
- medium saucepan
- wooden spoon
- electric hand whisk
- serving spoon

A typical serving contains (based on the max. number of people this recipe serves):

Calories	Sugar	Fat	Saturates	Salt
288	25g	16g	10g	0.2g
16%	29%	23%	50%	5%

of a child's guideline daily amount

Make the jelly base

Break up the sponge fingers

- Break up the sponge fingers and put them in the glasses

Chop the strawberries

- Remove the stalks from the strawberries
- Chop the strawberries into small pieces
- Put them in the glasses

Add the blueberries

- Put the blueberries in the glasses

Add raspberries

- Put the raspberries in the glasses too

Make the jelly

- Place the jelly squares in a mixing bowl
- Pour ½ pint of boiling water over them

Mix with fork until it has dissolved

- Keep mixing with a fork until all of the jelly has dissolved in the water

Pour it into a jug

Add cold water to make a pint

- Top up the jug to a pint with cold water

Pour the jelly mix into glasses

- Pour enough jelly into the glasses to cover the fruit and sponge

Push the fruit down into the jelly

- Use a fork to push the fruit down into the jelly

Put them in the fridge to set

- Put the glasses on a tray and then into the fridge
- The jelly needs at least an hour in the fridge to set

Make the custard

Add caster sugar to custard powder

- Put the caster sugar and custard powder into a bowl

Mix them together

- Mix them together using a whisk

Pour in some milk

- Add just a little milk

Whisk together

- Keep whisking until you make a thick paste

Boil the milk

- Pour the remaining milk into a saucepan and bring it to the boil on a medium heat

Add the custard and whisk

- When the milk begins to boil, add the custard paste
- Keep whisking until it thickens
- Turn off the heat

Allow the custard to cool

- Allow the custard to cool before pouring it into the glasses
- If the custard is too hot it will melt the jelly, but if it's too cold it will be too thick to pour!

Pour it in to the glasses

- When the custard has cooled, pour it into the glasses

Put them back in the fridge to set

- Put the trifles back in the fridge
- The trifles need at least 20–30 minutes to set

Finish & serve

Add icing sugar to the cream

- Add the icing sugar to the whipping cream in a mixing bowl

Whisk

- Whisk until you can make soft peaks in the cream

Spoon on top of the trifles

- When the custard has set, place a dollop of cream on top of each trifle

Spread it to the edges

- Spread the cream to the edges using a spoon

Add fruit on top

- Put extra fruit on top of the cream, to decorate

Dust the top with icing sugar

Serve

Image taken from video

Giant Cookies

Gigantic chocolate chip cookies, crispy on the outside, gooey in the middle. Great served with a glass of cold milk!

RATING 

Ingredients

- ½ an egg
- 140g soft brown sugar
- 60g butter, soft
- 20g self-raising flour
- 75g plain flour
- 20g cocoa powder
- a pinch of bicarbonate of soda
- 30ml semi-skimmed milk
- 100g chocolate chips

Utensils

- mixing bowl
- fork
- 2 small bowls
- food processor
- spatula
- measuring jug
- serving spoon
- baking tray
- wire rack

A typical serving contains (based on the max. number of people this recipe serves):

Calories	Sugar	Fat	Saturates	Salt
477	48g	22g	14g	0.7g
26%	56%	31%	70%	17%

of a child's guideline daily amount

Step 1 Make the cookie dough

Crack an egg into a bowl

- Pre-heat the oven to 160°C (310°F or gas mark 2)
- Crack the egg into a small bowl

Beat the egg

- Beat the egg thoroughly with a fork

Split the beaten egg in half

- Divide the beaten egg equally between the 2 small bowls – you will only use the egg in one of the bowls

Add the brown sugar and butter

- Put the sugar and butter into a food processor – you can also use a hand-held electric whisk for this

Add the ½ egg

- Add the beaten egg from one of the 2 bowls

Mix thoroughly

- Mix the ingredients thoroughly for a couple of minutes

Scrape

- Use a plastic spatula to scrape any unmixed ingredients from the side of the bowl

Mix again

- Mix again

Add the other ingredients

- Add the self-raising flour, plain flour and cocoa powder

Add the bicarbonate of soda

- Add a pinch of bicarbonate of soda

Add the milk

- Finally, add the milk to the mixture

Mix again

- Mix thoroughly again

Scrape the sides again and mix

- Again, use a plastic spatula to scrape any unmixed ingredients from the side of the bowl

Add the chocolate chips

- When the ingredients are thoroughly combined, add the chocolate chips

Pulse to mix

- Just pulse it to mix in the chocolate chips, but not chop them up

That's it!

- The mix will last for up to a week in the fridge

Step 2 Bake the cookies

Spoon the mix into 4 equal dollops

- Separate the mix into 4 dollops on the baking tray
- If you want to make more cookies, just make smaller dollops

Flatten them slightly

- Flatten the dollops slightly with a wet fork to help them spread out
- Make sure you leave a gap (of about 5cm) between each one as they will settle and spread out as they are cooking

Put the cookies in the oven to cook

- Bake for 10–15 minutes at 160°C (310°F or gas mark 2)

Leave to cool on the tray

- When cooked, leave the cookies to stand and cool for 5 minutes on the tray
- Turn off the oven
- The cookies will still be soft when they come out of the oven – if you try and move them too soon they will break up!

Transfer them to a wire rack

- Carefully transfer the cookies to a wire rack to cool completely

Serve when cool

- When the cookies are cool enough they are ready to serve

image taken from video

Lemon Loaf

A zingy, lemony, soft loaf cake with mixed peel and chopped nuts. A simple recipe that works every time.

PREP TIME **25** MINUTES

COOK TIME **1** HOUR

MAKES **6–8** SLICES

RATING

Ingredients

- softened butter for greasing
- 90g self-raising flour
- pinch of baking powder
- 75g soft brown sugar
- 25g mixed peel (optional)
- 15g mixed nuts (optional)
- 2 unwaxed lemons (juice and zest)
- 1 egg
- 75ml sunflower oil
- 40g icing sugar (sieved)

Utensils

- 450g loaf tin or tin foil bread trays
- baking paper
- kitchen scissors
- sieve
- medium mixing bowl
- silicone spatula/spoon
- cheese grater
- small chopping knife
- fork
- small mixing bowl
- wire rack
- bread knife

A typical serving contains (based on the max. number of people this recipe serves):

Calories	Sugar	Fat	Saturates	Salt
266	32g	18g	3.0g	0.4g
20%	38%	26%	15%	10%

of a child's guideline daily amount

Prepare the tin

Line the tin

- Lay the loaf tin on its side on the baking paper, making sure that the top of the tin is lined up with one edge of the paper

Roll it onto its base

- Roll the tin onto its base

Then onto other side

- Then roll the tin onto its other side (this will show you how wide the paper should be)

Cut to size

- Cut the paper to size

Repeat lengthways

- Do the same process to measure the length

Cut in from the corners

- Cut the paper in towards the centre from the corners

Butter the tin

- Grease the loaf tin with softened butter (this will help the baking paper stick to the sides)

Push the baking paper into the tin

- Line the base and sides of the tin with the baking paper, making sure you press it into all the corners
- Add more butter if it's not sticking properly

Step 2 Make the mix

Sieve the flour and baking powder

- Sieve the flour and baking power together into a medium mixing bowl

Add the dry ingredients to the flour

- Add the brown sugar to the flour (and the mixed peel and mixed nuts if you are including these)

Mix together

- Mix all the dry ingredients together in the bowl using a silicone spatula

Grate the lemon zest

- Grate the zest from the lemons, making sure you tap out all of the zest from the grater

Halve the lemons

- Cut the lemons in half

Squeeze the juice from the lemons

- Squeeze out the juice through a sieve into a small mixing bowl (this will make sure there are no pips in the juice)

Crack the egg into the lemon juice

- Crack the egg into the bowl with the lemon juice

Beat the egg

- Beat the egg into the lemon juice using the fork

Add the oil and beat

- Add the oil and beat it together with the egg and lemon juice mixture

Add the lemon zest and egg mix

- Add the lemon zest and egg mix to the bowl

Mix well

- Mix everything together thoroughly until you have a batter consistency

Pour it into the cake tin

- Pour the mix into the cake tin

Step 3

Bake the cake

Put the loaf in the oven

- Bake the loaf in an oven, pre-heated to 170°C (325°F or gas mark 3) for about 1 hour

Test the loaf is cooked

- After an hour, check whether the loaf is cooked by piercing it with a knife to the centre
- If it comes out clean then it's cooked–if not bake it for a little longer

When cooked, leave to cool

- When it's cooked, take the loaf out of the oven and leave it to cool slightly
- Turn off the oven

Turn the loaf out onto a wire rack

- When slightly cooled, carefully turn out the loaf onto a wire rack

Remove the baking paper

- Remove the baking paper and leave the loaf to cool for at least an hour

Cut into 2cm-thick slices

- When the cake has cooled, dust it with icing sugar
- Use a bread knife to cut the loaf into slices that are each about 2cm-thick

Serve